Edward Walford

Tales of Our Great Families

Vol. 1

Edward Walford

Tales of Our Great Families
Vol. 1

ISBN/EAN: 9783337088606

Printed in Europe, USA, Canada, Australia, Japan

Cover: Foto ©ninafisch / pixelio.de

More available books at **www.hansebooks.com**

OF

OUR GREAT FAMILIES.

BY

EDWARD WALFORD, M.A.

AND LATE SCHOLAR OF BALLIOL COLL., OXFORD.

AUTHOR OF
"THE COUNTY FAMILIES,"
&c., &c.

FIRST SERIES.
IN TWO VOLUMES.

VOL. I.

LONDON:
HURST AND BLACKETT, PUBLISHERS,
13, GREAT MARLBOROUGH STREET.
1877.

All rights reserved.

PREFACE.

UNDER the title of "Tales of our Great Families," I have ventured to publish a series of narratives relating to the families of the titled and untitled nobility of this country, in the hope of amusing my readers with materials which for twenty years I have been gleaning from various sources, and which have grown so rapidly in my hands that my only difficulty seems to lie in selecting amid such an *embarras de richesses*. If it be not literally true that every house, whether high or low, has its "skeleton in the closet," at all events the past history of most of our ancient houses is replete with incidents which, however artlessly they may be told, will certainly make good the adage that "truth is stranger than fiction."

In treating of these matters I wish by way of preface to remark that my readers must not always look for *novelty*. I shall often, I know, be telling a "thrice-told tale;" for in the anecdotal writings of Horace Walpole, Mrs. Delany, Sir Nathaniel Wraxall, the Hon. Grantley Berkeley, Captain Gronow, Lord William Lennox, the late Duke of Buckingham, and Dr. Doran, I have a constant well from which to draw supplies. It will be possible, however, to recast these materials and those taken from other sources, and to mould them all into one harmonious whole, which, I trust, may not be found devoid of interest. I am treading on delicate ground, and I am conscious that here and there I may wound the tender susceptibilities of descendants and relatives of the personages whom I may bring upon the stage. But to these I would say that the lives of the members of our old historic houses are themselves historic, and that I have a full right to wake up the memory of what already stands recorded against them in the gossiping pages of Sir Nathaniel Wraxall or Horace Walpole, unless I have reason to believe that the stories I tell are untrue. If these papers shall have any result beyond the amusement of the leisure hours of those who take an interest in the fates and fortunes of our "Great Families," I feel no doubt that, on the whole, that influence will not be of an injurious nature, and that I shall not be justly chargeable with lowering the esteem in which I hope that the aristocracy of this land will long be held. My papers may *occasionally* help to show up a pretender and a charlatan in his true colours; but in the long run they will be found, I am confident, rather to enhance the interest which attaches to that body at whose head stand the titled names of Howard and Stanley, Talbot and Herbert, Courtenay and Cavendish, and the equally noble though untitled name of Scrope.

It should be stated that some of these Tales have appeared in the columns of "The Queen," while a few others saw the light in "Chambers' Journal" and "The City Press."

CONTENTS

OF

THE FIRST VOLUME.

	Page
The Lady Blanche Arundell of Wardour . . .	1
The Two Fair Gunnings	19
The Thellussons	41
The Noble House of Cecil	52
Laurence, Earl Ferrers	83
The Duchess of Kingston	105
The Drummonds, Earls of Perth . . .	130
The Three Miss Walpoles	147
The Wooing of Sir Heneage Finch . . .	168
The Ducal House of Leeds	183
An Episode in the History of the Cathcarts .	194
An Episode in the Noble House of Hastings .	207
Thomas Pitt, Lord Camelford . . .	215
An Episode in the Earldom of Pembroke .	235
The Rise of the Rothschilds . . .	250
An Episode in the House of Harley . .	269
The Bad Lord Stourton	282
Benjamin, Lord Bloomfield	298

TALES

OF

OUR GREAT FAMILIES.

THE LADY BLANCHE ARUNDELL
OF WARDOUR.

FEW of the ruined homes of our ancient families are surrounded with a brighter halo of interest than the old Castle of Wardour, which stands on the south-western border of Wiltshire, about half way between Salisbury and Shaftesbury; and few heroines of our own country have earned a fairer name for bravery, courage, and devotion in the hour of danger than the Lady Blanche Arundell of Wardour.

By birth the Lady Blanche came of a noble and distinguished race, the Somersets, at that time Earls of Worcester, now Marquises of

Worcester and Dukes of Beaufort. She was the sixth out of seven daughters who were born to Edward, the fourth Earl, by his wife Elizabeth, daughter of Francis, Earl of Huntingdon; and early in the reign of James I. she became the wife of Thomas, second Lord Arundell of Wardour, whose father, known far and wide in his day as "the Valiant," had been created Lord Arundell of Wardour, and also a Count of the Holy Roman Empire on account of his gallantry at the siege of Gran in Hungary, where, serving under the banner of the Emperor Rudolph of Germany, he captured the Turkish standard with his own hands.

The Emperor's patent or charter (A.D. 1695) states expressly that the title was conferred on him because "he had behaved himself manfully in the field, and also had shown great proof of valour in the assaulting of divers cities and castles, especially in forcing the water-tower near Strigonium, when he took from the Turks their banner with his own hand." This honour was extended to every one of his children and descendants of either sex, so that every infant who is born an Arundell is born also a count or countess of the Roman Empire. Collins, in his Peerage, Vol. V. p. 119, gives an amusing account of the reason which led to his being created an English Baron also. "On his return home, a controversy arising among the Peers whether that dignity, so conferred by a foreign potentate, should be allowed here as to place and precedence, or any other privilege, it occasioned a warm dispute, which is mentioned by Camden in his History of Queen Elizabeth. The Queen, being asked her opinion of the case, is reported to have answered that 'there was a close tie of affection between the prince and subject, and that, as chaste wives should have no glances but for their own spouses, so should faithful subjects keep their eyes at home, and not gaze on foreign coronets; that she, for her part, did not care that her sheep should wear a stranger's mark, or dance after the whistle of every foreigner.'" The consequence was that the precedence claimed on account of this foreign honour was disallowed. King James, however, soon after his accession, made amends for Elizabeth's jealousy by creating him Lord Arundell, of Wardour, in the county of Wilts.

In 1639 Lady Blanche's husband succeeded to his father's peerage, just as the Puritan storm was gathering which was destined to burst on the head of King Charles I. and of all his devoted and loyal-heared followers and subjects, whether Protestants or Roman Catholics.

In the history of the Civil War which is usually known as "The Great Rebellion," few episodes are more touching than that of the siege, capture, and recapture of the Castle of Wardour; but I must first say a word or two about the castle itself.

The manor of Wardour or Warder, as may be seen in Sir R. C. Hoare's "History of Wiltshire," was in early times the property of a family named St. Martin; but the castle itself appears to have been built in the reign of Richard II., the last of the Plantagenets, by John, Lord Lovel of Tichmarsh. The Lovels inhabited it for only three generations, as it was sold on the death of the last-named nobleman's grandson in 1494, the next heir to the estate finding himself involved in great difficulties by his adherence to the failing cause of the Red Rose of Lancaster.

The property of the Lovels was at that time as extensive as any in the kingdom, and it must be owned that Lord Lovel showed great taste in the selection of a site for his castle, which is thus described in the *Gentleman's Magazine* for August, 1867: "It stands on a flat plateau, supported by high wooded banks on every side, except on the south-west, where the ground slopes down to the park and the lake, admitting a glowing sun to light and warm the haughty building. A spot of greater beauty could hardly have been found amongst all the scenes afforded by that peculiarly rich part of Wiltshire where it marches with the Dorsetshire border. On the eastern side, flanked by two strong square towers, was the great entrance, over which is still to be read a Latin inscription relating how the castle came into the hands of the Arundells."

We learn that after the Lovels, its next owners were the Touchets, Lords Audley (afterwards Earls of Castlehaven), to whom it was given by Edward IV. in reward of their adherence to the White Rose of York. The Touchets, however, did not long hold it; for the second of that line who owned it, having been taken in arms against Henry VII. at the battle of Blackheath, was beheaded on Tower Hill. His estates, of course, were confiscated; and Wardour Castle, after having been held for a short time by Sir Fulke Greville, was purchased by Sir John Arundell, of Llanherne, in Cornwall, who presented it to his second son, Thomas, who married a sister of Catharine Howard, the fifth wife of Henry VIII. Attaching himself, however, very warmly to the Duke of Somerset, in the next reign he shared the Duke's fate, and perished on the scaffold.

The estates of Wardour were now again confiscated, and granted to the Earl of Pembroke, whose seat at Wilton lay but a few miles distant, and who, no doubt, was glad to join Wardour on to his own domain. However, in the course of a few years the Earl resolved to sell it, when it was repurchased by Sir Matthew Arundell, whose eldest son was the hero of Hungary, and became the first Lord Arundell of Wardour.

The chief features of the building, as it was erected by Lord Lovel, still remain to the present day. It forms an irregular quadrangle, flanked at the four corners by four large main towers. Above the entrance are the large windows of what was the great banqueting hall; they still remain, presenting but a few indications of the rich tracery with which they once were filled. The form of the court was a hexagon. Each tower had a staircase of its own, and a door leading into the courtyard—I can scarcely call a six-sided space a quadrangle—in the centre of which was a deep well. Besides these, there was one principal staircase, leading up from the court into the great hall. Parts of these staircases still remain, but not a floor or a roof now stands entire; and the great banqueting hall, which once resounded with song and music, and was gay with banners and tapestry, is now roofless and bare, inhabited only by owls and jackdaws, which find a home in the ivy that clusters thick and dark around the tenantless walls. But it is time that I should hasten on to tell the story of the siege of Wardour Castle, and of the heroism of the Lady Blanche Arundell.

Thomas, the second Lord Arundell, having always shown the warmest and most loyal attachment to the royal cause, as soon as the Civil War broke out, joined King Charles I. with a regiment of horse, which he had raised and equipped at his own expense, and was soon as much distinguished by his bravery as by his fidelity. Foreseeing the vengeance which his loyalty would be sure to call down on his house and family should the cause of the Roundheads and Puritans triumph, before joining the King's standard he exacted from his wife a promise that, if his castle should be attacked in his absence, it should be defended to the very last extremity. How faithfully the Lady Blanche redeemed the promise which she made to her lord, as he tore himself from her embrace on quitting Wardour for the last time, is proved by the written testimony of both friends and enemies.

I will not waste time by dwelling long on the picture which that parting scene must have presented, beyond saying that it is enough to have inspired half our painters and poets. There is the gate of the old grey castle, in deep shadow, while the rays of the afternoon sun light up the opposite bank with a golden glow, which catches the plumes of the cavaliers and dances on their long flowing hair, as their horses prance and toss their heads impatient to start on their march towards Lansdowne Hill and Bath; and the first of the troops are already defiling from the castle yard. The standard of the Arundells (sable, six swallows, *hirondelles,* arg.) waves in the breeze, and the ringing bugle, the tramping of the horses, the gay colouring of their housings, and the bright equipments of their riders, all combine to form a brilliant contrast to that group of anxious and loving faces that cluster round the great doorway, seeking the last embrace and the last words of those dear ones on whom they know and feel they are possibly now to look for the last time.

Alas, for the Lady Blanche! Her fair face, crowned with locks whitening with her sixtieth summer, is raised to meet the lips of her true lord, who lowers his casque and stoops from his charger to give her the last kiss. Alas indeed for her! for, whatever fate may be in store for the dear ones of her companion ladies, that kiss and that look of her husband was destined to be the very last. A few short months, and her husband would come back indeed, but a corpse.

He would come back with glory and honour to Wardour, but not to her; he would come back to his grave in the church hard by. He would come back; but it would not be in his power to give her that which she coveted most of all things in this world—the smile of approval, the thought of which was to be her solace through the weary and toilsome hours of the coming siege. There too stands her son's wife, Cicely, the daughter of Sir Henry Compton, of Brambletye House, Sussex, and widow of Sir John Fermor, young and delicate, and half heart-broken at having to part with her husband, the father of her three young children, who cling to her, half sobbing, half smiling, puzzled at the grief of their mother and their grandmother, and at the pretty sight of the warlike cavalcade.

As Lord Arundell rode away, gazing back on his home, well may we imagine that the Lady Blanche would raise her hands to heaven and vow before saints and angels that she would keep the word which she had given to her lord, and that the vow was echoed back firmly and quietly by Cicely, and somewhat more loudly and emphatically by the fifty serving men who were to form the garrison, and the bevy of waiting maids who stood crying in the background. Though sixty years old, she joined to the firmness and wisdom of that age the energy of youth and the spirit of a Somerset; and it was without the smallest signs of fear or of any weak emotion that on the 2nd of May, 1643, she received the news that the Puritan leader, Sir Edward Hungerford, was at her doors, and that, in the name of the Parliament, he required admittance in order to search for cavaliers and " malignants."

It is needless to say that Sir Edward's demand was disdainfully refused, and that he saw enough to convince him that it would be no easy task to effect an entry into that castle in its owner's absence. He therefore sent for Colonel Strode and some troops under his command, which raised the force at his disposal to a total of thirteen hundred men. He then sent a messenger to the Lady Blanche, demanding the surrender of the castle in due form; but the only reply that he received was that " she had a command from her lord to keep it, and would obey that command."

For the last time on that evening, Lady Arundell looked out in freedom from her chamber in the tower; and it must have been with a heavy heart that she gazed on the lake below her windows—that lake which still spreads its peaceful waters to reflect the glowing sunsets—

and noted the splashing of the carp as they played on its surface, and the song of the blackbird, the thrush, and the cuckoo. But, together with that heavy heart, she nursed and inwardly cherished the firm resolve that she would dare and do all that woman could and might, for the sake of her husband who had gone to the war.

Late at night, a harsher sound must have been borne on the breeze to her ears—the rattle of heavy guns and of soldiers escorting them along the road that wound through the woods. The Puritans, at all events, had lost no time, for in the morning her waiting-maid aroused her by the news that the guns were already in position to bear full upon the walls. Unfortunately, too, for herself and for Wardour, the castle was placed in a situation chosen rather for its beauty than for its military capabilities. It lay low, and the ground, rising around it on three out of the four sides, gave her enemies a great advantage, of which the Roundheads were not slow to avail themselves.

Next day commenced a fierce cannonade, and the first shot fell with deadly force in the banqueting hall, where it cruelly damaged the great chimney-piece, richly carved in dark red marble, and said to have been worth £2000 even at that time—a far larger sum than that which is now represented by those figures. Portions of this mantel-piece are still preserved in the grounds, worked into a sort of rockery, and some of the cannon balls have also been kept as relics and memorials of the siege. For six long days and nights, almost without intermission, the battery continued to hurl its deadly missiles on the besieged garrison, who stoutly and valiantly rejected the conditions proffered over and over again by the Roundheads, who promised quarter to the ladies alone and not to the men under arms. The number within the walls was small, for out of the fifty males only twenty-five were trained fighting men; and had it not been for the assistance of the maid-servants, who steadily loaded their muskets, they would have been exhausted with fatigue and want of sleep before they could have held out long enough to obtain honourable terms for all.

On the fourth or fifth day of the siege two mines were sprung. The first did but little damage, as fortunately it proved to be outside the walls of the castle; but the second, which exploded inside one of the smaller vaults, greatly shook the building, and showed that the fabric was in danger of destruction. Still, however, the Lady Blanche resolved not to yield; and it was not until the sixth day, when the rebels brought petards and applied them to the great door, and balls of wild-fire to throw in at the windows, that the gallant defender found herself obliged to " sound a parley."

Thus reduced to the last straits, she agreed to a surrender, but on condition of obtaining quarter for all within the castle. It was also agreed that the wearing apparel of the ladies should be at their own disposal, and they should be allowed six serving men to attend upon them wherever their captors should dispose of them; and it was further agreed that all the furniture in the castle should be safe from plunder.

Finding themselves, however, in possession of the castle walls, these " saints of the Lord" did not feel bound to observe any of their promises except the first. " Faith is not to be kept with heretics," it would appear, is a principle current in society at large, and acted on by many others besides those whom the world calls " Romish bigots." It is true that they spared the lives of the gallant defenders of the castle, though the latter had used their guns and cross-bows so well as to kill above sixty of the besieging force. The ladies and the three children were at once led off as prisoners of war to Shaftesbury, just over the Dorsetshire border, where they had the mortification of seeing five cartloads of the spoils of Wardour driven in triumph through the streets of the town on their way to Dorchester, which was then in the hands of the Parliamentary army.

After a time, considering, or pretending to consider, that the captive ladies and children were not safe at Shaftesbury, the rebels proposed to remove them to Bath, where the plague was then raging, and where the " saints" probably hoped that death would do the work which they dared not try with their own hands. But here the high spirit of Lady Arundell was fully roused, and, as she lay at the time in bed, worn out with fatigue and anxiety, she refused to be removed unless she was dragged by actual main force. Dreading the unpopularity which such severity would draw down upon their cause in the Western counties, where the name of Arundell was held in high esteem, at length the " saints" abandoned their designs; so they contented themselves with wresting from Cicely Arundell her two little boys, aged nine and seven respectively, whom they considered such objects of alarm that they sent them under a strong guard to Dorchester.

Meantime my readers may wish to know how it fared with the fabric which had stood the siege, and with the estates that surrounded it. If so, I will tell them.

Sir Edward Hungerford and his troops, out of pure revenge and spite, laid waste the whole place with a frantic zeal, the effects of which are felt down to the present day. They tore up the park railings several miles in extent, let loose or killed the red and fallow deer—which have never since been replaced—burnt the park lodges and entrances, and cut down the trees, which they sold for fourpence and sixpence apiece, though they must have been worth as many pounds. They drove away all the horses and cattle, and even cut to pieces and sold as waste metal the leaden pipes which conveyed water underground to the Castle; and, in short, it is computed by local antiquaries that the havoc which they caused would scarcely be repaired for a hundred thousand pounds. Sir Edward Hungerford placed the Castle under the command of Colonel Ludlow, who held it from May 1643 to the March of the following year.

Just at this time of Ludlow's taking possession, news was brought to Wardour that Lord Arundell, the husband of the Lady Blanche, had died at Oxford of wounds which he had received at the battle of Lansdowne. A fortnight had scarcely elapsed when his son, young Lord

Arundell, the husband of Cicely, appeared before the walls, and summoned Ludlow and his crew to deliver up the place to him, " for his Majesty's use." This summons was of course refused ; and, burning with rage at his father's death, his mother's capture, and his children's imprisonment, he withdrew for a time to collect materials for the siege of his own castle. Early in the following year, accordingly, he sat down before it, determining to retake it, either by siege or by blockade. At length, despairing of being able to effect his object by any less violent means, he resolved to blow up the towers and walls rather than to leave it in the hands of the rebels. Accordingly, in the middle of the month of March, he sprang beneath it a mine which shattered its walls and western towers, and did so much damage also to the stores of corn and other provisions, that the garrison found themselves reduced to only four days' rations. Seeing at length that all hope was at an end, Colonel Ludlow capitulated, on terms which *were* observed by the Royalists, and the Castle came back again into the hands of its rightful owners :

> "And Bertram's right and Bertram's might
> Did meet on Ellangowan height."

But the fabric came back into the hands of

the noble and gallant Arundells sadly shorn of its chief ornaments, and of all that makes a house to be a home; and bitter indeed must have been the feelings of the young Lord Arundell when he once again entered the well-known halls, and gazed upon the bare walls of the despoiled rooms, which for ten long weary months had been tenanted by the rough and sour soldiers of the Parliament, instead of by his own gentle wife and his noble-hearted mother. However, he did return; and the family once more occupied such portions of the Castle as could be put into a habitable condition.

Just a hundred years ago, when the old Castle had seen a hundred and thirty years of ruin and desolation, a new and noble mansion, in the Classical style, which now bears the name of Wardour Castle, was built by the then Lord Arundell, about a mile from the ancient site, where the old grey walls rising proudly out of a wilderness of dark foliage beside a lake, and what once was a garden and a " pleasaunce," still tell the tale of their defence by the hands of the Lady Blanche Arundell.

And what about Lady Blanche herself? She survived for some six years or more the loss of her husband and the siege of his Castle. On her release from captivity at Shaftesbury, she retired to Winchester, where she lived in seclusion, leading a life of piety and charity; and there she ended her days in October, 1649, having lived long enough to add to her other griefs by mourning the fate of the sovereign whom her husband had served so loyally. The fine old parish church of Tisbury, adjoining the park of Wardour, now holds all that is mortal of the Lady Blanche Arundell.

It is some satisfaction, though a poor one at the best, to know that Providence in the end punished the proud house of Hungerford, one of whose members had taken so active a part in bringing about the desolation of the fair Castle of Wardour. Those who wish to know how justice overtook the Hungerfords, will do well to consult that storehouse of amusing anecdote, " The Vicissitudes of Families," by Sir Bernard Burke.

THE TWO FAIR GUNNINGS.

CAN it be that female beauty has degenerated in England during the last century? Such a decadence seems improbable, nay, impossible, in a country where the fair sex avail themselves so plentifully of Nature's two great beautifiers, fresh air and cold water! And yet, which among our celebrated beauties of the present day, whose photographs may be seen in every stationer's window, can boast of having excited one half of the *furore* created by the two fair Miss Gunnings, who took the London world of fashion by storm in the year 1751, and turned the West End almost mad?

These ladies, whose beauty and whose names are familiar to every reader of Horace Walpole and of books of contemporary anecdote and biography, were sisters, of plain Irish extraction, wholly without fortune; and their only title to aristocratic family was the fact that they were distantly related to an Irish baronet of the name. The sudden appearance of these stars in the heaven of London fashion caused so great a sensation that even the staid rules of a Court drawing room at St. James's were defied by a mob of noble gentlemen and ladies clambering upon chairs and tables to get a look at them.

Walpole speaks of them as being "scarce gentlewomen, but by their mother;" but this somewhat ill-natured remark is scarcely true. The family of Gunning could hardly be said to be aristocratic in name or in lineage, but still it was respectable enough; and on their mother's side Maria and Elizabeth Gunning might fairly boast that the blood of the Plantagenets ran in their veins.

All that the Heralds' College can tell us of the Gunning family—beyond the fact that a member of it, having been British Minister at the Courts of Berlin and St. Petersburg, was raised to a baronetcy about a century ago—is that it was divided into two branches, which possessed in the reign of Henry VIII. considerable estates in the counties of Kent, Somerset, and Gloucester, and that one of the Kentish Gunnings, in the reign of James I., settled in Ireland, where he became the ancestor of the Gunnings of Castle Coote, in the county of Roscommon. One of these, a Mr. John Gunning, by his marriage with the Hon. Bridget Bourke, a daughter of Viscount Bourke, of Mayo, had, along with a son who became a general in the army, and who distinguished himself at the battle of Bunker's Hill, three fair daughters, who were said to rival the Three Graces. Two of these came to London, like many other portionless girls before and after their time, to push their way in the world of fashion, their "faces" being their "fortunes," in the words of the well-known song:

"My face is my fortune, Sir, she said."

The third, and youngest, appears to have settled down quietly in matrimonial life, in the south of Ireland; but she does not come within the scope of this paper, which I intend to devote to the career of her two sisters.

A letter concerning the Gunnings, written by the parish clerk of Hemingford Grey, in Huntingdonshire, to Mr. James Madden, of Cole House, Fulham, is worth transcribing, less for the sake of the information it contains, which is, for the most part, an incorrect version of well-known facts, than on account of the amusing self-importance of the writer. I follow his orthography:

"Sir,

"I take the Freedom in wrighting to you, from an information of Mr. Warrinton, that you would be Glad to have the account of my Townswoman the Notefied, the Famis, Beautifull Miss Gunnings. Born at Hemingford Grey, tho they left the Parish before I had Knoledge Enough to Remember them, and I was born in 32 (1732). But I will give you the Best account I can, which I believe is Better than any man in the Country besides Myself, tho I have not the Birth Register for so long a Date, and since Dr Dickens is dead, I dont know where it is, but the Best account I Can Give you is, Elizth. the Eldest, married to his Grace the Duke of Hamilton, after his Decease to the Duke of Arguile; the second, Mary, to the Viscount of Coventre; the third I never knew ritely to home, but I beleeve to some privett Gentleman. I Rember a many years ago at least 30, seeing her picture in a print shop, I believe in St. Poul's Churchyard, as follows:

"the youngest of these Beauties here we have in vue,
so like in person to the other two,
ho Ever views her features and her fame,
will see at once that Gunning is her Name."

which is the Best account I Can give you of these three; but then there was two more, which perhaps you don't know anything about, which I will give you the true Mortalick register off, from a black mavel which lies in our chancel, as follows:—Sophia Gunning, the youngest of four daughters, all born at Hemmingford, in Huntingdonshire, to John Gunning, Esq.; died an infant, 1737. Lissy Gunning, his fifth daughter, born in Ireland; died December 31, 1752, aged 8 years 10 months. 'Suffer little children and forbid them not to come unto me, for of such is the kingdom of heaven.'—Matt. xix. 14. This, Sir, is the Truest and Best Information I Can Give you, or can Get, and if this is of any use to you, I should be much obliged to you to let me have a line or two from you, that I may be satisfied that it was not in vain.

"And am, Sir,
"Your most obedient and humble servant,
"Wm. Criswell.
"Hemmingford Grey, August 14, 1796."

But little is known of Catherine, the third Miss Gunning, in the annals of fashion; but I can so far supplement the information of Mr. William Criswell, as to tell your readers that the "privett gentleman" alluded to was Robert Travis, Esq., to whom Catherine Gunning was married in 1769, and who had a daughter who in the next generation kept up the fame of the family for personal beauty.

Whatever may have been the original fortune and estate of John Gunning, of Castle Coote, Ireland, the progenitor of "the two fair Gunnings," it would seem that at the time when they were just budding into womanhood, their mother, the Hon. Mrs Gunning, seriously contemplated sending them to seek their fortunes upon the stage. Walpole more than once alludes to this intention; and the circumstances under which the lovely sisters were presented at Dublin Castle the year before their *début* in London, would seem to give colour to the supposition. The Gunnings were on intimate terms with Thomas Sheridan, at that time manager of the Dublin Theatre; and Mrs Gunning, wishing to present her daughters to the Earl of Harrington, then Lord-Lieutenant, consulted Sheridan how could she procure the necessary dresses, which she had not the means to purchase. The difficulty was overcome by Sheridan arraying the distressed beauties out of the resources of the stage wardrobe; and so Maria and Elizabeth Gunning made their first courtesies to the Lord-Lieutenant attired as Lady Macbeth and Juliet, and, as tradition states, looked most lovely. I wish it did not also state that, when they became great ladies, they proved forgetful of former kindness in their time of need on the part of the warm-hearted, improvident Sheridan.

The first mention that we find of the fair Gunnings as the "Belles of the season" in London, is in a letter from Horace Walpole in June, 1751, when he speaks of them as "two Irish girls of no fortune, who make more noise than any of their predecessors since the days of Helen, and who are declared the handsomest women alive." The fastidious Horace "was willing to allow the truth of the statement if they were both taken together;" though he adds by way of qualification, that "singly he has seen much handsomer women than either of them." How this can be, however, is not clear to my dull comprehension.

There can be no doubt of the sensation caused by the two fair Gunnings wherever they went about London. They could not take a walk in the park, or spend an evening at Vauxhall, without being followed by such mobs as to force them to retire and go home. One day when the sisters visited Hampton Court, the housekeeper, whether in sport or in earnest, showed the company who were "lionising" the place into the room where the Miss Gunnings were sitting, instead of into the apartment known as the "Beauty room," with the significant remark, "These are the beauties, ladies."

The fair sisters, the elder of whom had barely completed her eighteenth year at the time of which I am speaking, as may easily be imagined, did not long retain the humble patronymic which they had brought with them from Ireland, and had rendered so famous. Elizabeth, the younger sister, drew the first prize in the matrimonial lottery; and the story of her courtship and marriage had best perhaps be told in Horace Walpole's own words, which lets us into a scene in Mayfair Chapel in the days when marriages not *à la mode* were solemnised there. The old gossip writes to his friend Sir Horace Mann, at Florence, under date Feb. 27, 1752:

"The event which has made the most noise since my last is the wedding of the younger Miss Gunning. . . . About six weeks ago the Duke of Hamilton, the very reverse of the Earl [of Coventry], but debauched, extravagant, and equally damaged in his fortune and in his person, fell in love with the youngest at a masquerade, and determined to marry her in the spring. About a fortnight since, at an immense assembly at Lord Chesterfield's, made to show [off] the house, which is really most magnificent, the

Duke made love at one end of the room, while he was playing at pharaoh (*i.e.*, faro) with the other: that is, he saw neither the bank nor his own cards, which were of £300 each. He soon lost a thousand. I own I was so little a professor in love that I thought this parade looked ill for the poor girl, and could not conceive, if he was so much engaged with his mistress as to disregard such sums, why he played at all. However, two nights afterwards, being left alone with her he found himself so impatient that he sent for a parson. The doctor refused to perform the ceremony without either a license or a ring. The Duke swore he would send for the archbishop. At last they were married with a ring of the bed curtain, at half an hour after twelve, at Mayfair Chapel. The Scotch are enraged; the women mad that so much beauty has had its effect; and, what is most silly, my Lord Coventry declares that now he will marry the other. The Duchess was presented on Friday. The crowd was so great that even the noble mob in the drawing room clambered into chairs and on tables to get a look at her. There are mobs at their door to see them get into their chairs; and people go early to get places at the theatres when it is known that they will be there."

A few weeks after the marriage, the Duke of

Hamilton conducted his lovely bride to the home of his ancestors; and so widely spread was the fame of the beautiful Duchess, even in those days when railways, penny postage, and daily newspapers were things unknown, that, when they stopped one night at a Yorkshire inn during their journey, "seven hundred people sat up all night in and about the house merely to see the Duchess get into her post-chaise the next morning."

There can be little doubt that Elizabeth Gunning's first marriage was prompted by ambition: it could hardly have been a happy one, if we may credit Walpole's account of the Hamilton *ménage*. "The Duchess of Hamilton's history," says he, "is not unentertaining. The Duke of Hamilton is the abstract of Scotch pride. He and the Duchess, at their own house, walk in to dinner before their company, sit together at the upper end of their own table, eat off the same plate, and drink to nobody beneath the rank of an earl. Would not one wonder how they could get anybody, either above or below that rank, to dine with them at all?" It is indeed a marvel how such a host could find guests of any degree sufficiently wanting in self-respect to sit at his table and endure his pompous insolence—the insolence of an innately vulgar mind, which, unhappily, is sometimes to be met even in the most exalted rank of life.

Let us now for the present leave Elizabeth Duchess of Hamilton to the enjoyment of her conjugal felicity in the congenial society of her stately spouse, and see what had meanwhile befallen her sister Maria.

Maria Gunning, the elder and according to the general opinion the loveliest of the two sisters, on her first introduction to the *beau monde* of London was followed by a long train of aristocratic and noble admirers, among whom was the Earl of Coventry; a grave young lord of the remains of the patriot breed, who long dangled after her. The wavering intention of the Earl was most probably decided by the example set him by one even of higher rank than himself; and the marriage of Elizabeth to his Grace of Hamilton was followed in less than three weeks by that of Maria to his Lordship. Our old friend Horace Walpole comments in a most characteristic manner upon the notoriety of the fair sisters. After recording the fact of their marriages, he continues, "There are two wretched women that are just as much talked of as the two beauties, a Miss Jefferies and a Miss Blandy; the one condemned for murdering her uncle, the other for the murder of her father." Lady

Gower, writing to a friend in the country shortly after the execution of these two criminals, and lamenting the lack of sufficient news to make her letter interesting says: "Since the two Misses were hanged (Blandy and Jefferies) and the other two Misses were married (the Gunnings), there is nothing at all talked of."

Shortly after their marriage the Earl and Countess of Coventry, accompanied by Lady Caroline Petersham—another celebrated beauty, whose charms were, however, at this period somewhat on the wane—paid a visit to France. But the standard of beauty must have been widely different in the two countries at that time, for the English belles, doubtless to their own extreme amazement, found themselves entirely at a discount in the French capital. "Our beauties," writes Walpole in October, 1752, "are returned, and have done no execution. The French would not conceive that Lady Caroline Petersham ever had been handsome, nor that my Lady Coventry has much pretence to be so now. Poor Lady Coventry," he continues, "was under piteous disadvantages; for, besides being very silly, ignorant of the world and good breeding, speaking no French, and suffered to wear neither red nor powder, she had that perpetual drawback upon her beauty; her lord, who is sillier in a wiser way, and as ignorant, speaking very little French himself, just enough to show how ill-bred he is." It would have been well for Lady Coventry if she had never been suffered to wear " red nor powder;" for it was to the lavish use of paint that the malady which caused her early death was attributed by her physicians.

The lovely Countess seems to have divided her time between her toilette and her amusements, On one occasion she exhibited to George Selwyn the costume which she was going to wear at an approaching *fête*. The dress was of blue silk, richly brocaded with silver spots of the size of a shilling. "And how do you think I shall look in it, Mr. Selwyn?" asked the self-satisfied beauty. "Why," replied he, "you will look like change for a guinea!"

Conspicuous in the list of this lady's adorers was Frederick St. John, Viscount Bolingbroke, *àpropos* of whom Walpole writes, March 2, 1754: "T'other night they danced minuets for the entertainment of the King at the masquerade, and then he sent for Lady Coventry to dance. It was quite like Herodias; and I believe, if he had offered a boon, she would have chosen the head of St. John—I think I told you of her passion for the young Lord Bolingbroke." A little later the Duke of Cumberland's admiration of Lady Coventry was the topic of conversation, according to that universal intelligencer from whom most of the gossip of the day has come down to us.

Many amusing stories are told of Lady Coventry's extreme silliness; one of the best of them is as follows: The old King (George II.) asked her one evening if she was not sorry that there were to be no more masquerades. She replied that "She was tired of them—indeed, that she was surfeited with most London sights; there was but one left that she wanted to see—and that was a coronation!" This wish (expressed with such *naïveté*) was not granted, for Lady Coventry died just a fortnight before the King.

The *prestige* of Lady Coventry's exceeding beauty attended her to the last. Only a few months before her death in 1760, she was so mobbed by a crowd of admiring plebeians while walking in the park, that the King ordered a guard to be always ready for the future, whenever Lady Coventry should be pleased to "take her walks abroad." Another letter-writer of the period, the Hon. J. West, gives an amusing description of the result of these precautions. "Her ladyship went to the park, and, pretending to be frightened, directly desired the assistance of the officer of the guard, who ordered twelve sergeants to walk abreast before her, and a sergeant and twelve men behind her, and in this pomp did the idiot walk about all the evening, with more mob about her than ever, as you may imagine; her sensible husband supporting her on one side, and Lord Pembroke on the other. This is at present the talk of the whole town."

Elizabeth Gunning, having become a widow in 1758, gave her hand, a twelvemonth later, to one Colonel John Campbell, then heir presumptive to the honours of the great ducal house of Argyll, and commenced married life for a second time under auspices even more brilliant and far happier than her first venture. Walpole writes of it as "A match that would not disgrace Arcadia. Her beauty has made enough sensation, and in some people's eyes is even improved. He has a most pleasing person, countenance, manner; and, if they could but carry to Scotland some of our sultry English weather, they might restore the ancient pastoral life, when fair kings and queens reigned at once over their subjects and their sheep."

It is a well-known fact, frequently mentioned by Chesterfield, Walpole, and other contemporary writers, that for the sake of Colonel Campbell, Elizabeth Gunning, in her year of widowhood, had rejected another ducal coronet, that of the Duke of Bridgewater.

But the career of the beautiful Countess was fast drawing to a close, and Walpole writes to a friend: "The kingdom of beauty is in as great disorder as the kingdom of Ireland. My Lady Pembroke looks like a ghost. My Lady Coventry is going to be one." Poor creature! The heartless wit spoke only too truly.

One of the last occasions on which we hear of her appearance in public was at the trial of Earl Ferrers, in the House of Lords, April 1760, for the murder of his steward. Walpole writes of this trial: "The seats of the peeresses were not near full, and most of the beauties absent; but, to the amazement of everybody, Lady Coventry was there, and, what surprised me much more, looked as well as ever. I sat next but one to her, and should not have asked her if she had been ill, yet they are positive she has few weeks to live. She and Lord Bolingbroke seemed to have different thoughts, and were acting over all the old comedy of eyes."

Walpole's description of her death-bed is a most melancholy one. "Poor Lady Coventry," he writes, "concluded her short race with the same attention to her looks. She lay constantly on a couch, with a pocket-glass in her hand; and when that told her how great the change was, she took to her bed. During the last fortnight she had no light in her room but the lamp of a tea-kettle, and at last took things in through the curtains of her bed, without suffering them to be withdrawn." The mob, who never quitted curiosity about her, went to the number of ten thousand only to see her coffin. Her married life extended over something more than eight years. She did not, however, pass away until she had borne to the earl three children; two daughters, and also a son, George William, who became the seventh Earl of Coventry, and lived for nine years in the present century.

I have before mentioned that Lady Coventry's early death was mainly attributed to her lavish use of cosmetics; and I find another terrible example of the same extraordinary infatuation in the pages from which I have already so largely quoted. Horace Walpole writes in 1762: "That pretty young woman, Lady Fortrose, Lady Harrington's daughter, is at the point of death, killed, like Lady Coventry and others, by white lead, of which nothing could cure her."

It will probably strike the reader of Horace Walpole's Letters that he speaks with undue harshness of Lady Coventry's ignorance and ill-breeding, when we consider the giddy height to which she had been raised from a life of obscurity, if not of poverty, at a very early age; the amount of adulation poured upon her by the highest personages in the land; and, above all, the facts that coarseness and ignorance were common failings among the aristocracy of that day.

At the time of her sister's death, in October, 1760, the Duchess of Hamilton was in such bad health that her physicians apprehended a rapid decline, and ordered her to pass the winter abroad. Walpole speaks of her at this time as possessing " but little remains of beauty;" her features, he adds, " were never so handsome as Lady Coventry's, and she has long been changed, though not yet, I think, above six-and-twenty; the other was but twenty-seven." The Duchess, however, recovered, and was one of the three ladies appointed to accompany the Princess Charlotte of Mecklenburg-Strelitz from Germany to England previous to her marriage with George III. It is said that when the young German bride arrived in sight of the palace of her future husband, she turned pale, and evinced such evident symptoms of terror as to force a smile from the Duchess of Hamilton, who sat by her side; upon which the young princess briskly remarked, "My dear duchess, you may laugh, for you have been married twice; but it is no joke to me."

The general respect in which the young Dowager Duchess of Hamilton was held at the time of her second marriage, forced an acknowledgment even from the censorious Walpole, that her merit was as conspicuous as her good fortune, and that the extraordinary sensation created by her beauty had not at all impaired the modesty of her behaviour. The Duchess of Hamilton became Duchess of Argyll in 1770, a change of title characteristically commented upon by Walpole, who observes that, "As she is not quite so charming as she was," he does not know "whether it is not better than to retain a title which put one in mind of her beauty." In 1776 she was created Baroness Hamilton, of Hamilton, in Leicestershire, in her own right. She was one of the Ladies of the Bedchamber to Queen Charlotte, who, jealous of her undoubted favour with the King, treated her so badly that at one time she contemplated resigning her post. The Duke consented that she should do so, on condition that he might dictate the letter of resignation. The letter was accordingly written, but the Duchess, greatly dissatisfied with the terms employed, which by no means expressed her feelings, added a postscript to this effect: "Though I wrote the letter, the Duke dictated it." Ultimately the affair was arranged by the Duchess retaining her place.

Elizabeth, Duchess of Hamilton and of Argyll, was the wife of two dukes, and the mother of four. By her first husband, she was mother of James, seventh duke, and of Douglas, eighth Duke of Hamilton; and by her second husband, of George, sixth duke, and of John, seventh Duke of Argyll. She died on the 20th December, 1790, and so terminated the history of the two fair Gunnings.

There is at Croome Court, the seat of the present Earl of Coventry, a fine portrait of Maria Gunning, and another of her "double-duchessed" sister; the latter was also painted by Sir Joshua Reynolds, and sat to other artists. At Inverary Castle, Argyllshire, the seat of the Duke of Argyll, there is an authentic full-length portrait of Elizabeth Gunning (his Grace's grand-mother) by Cotes, and another, also full-length, is to be seen at Hamilton Palace. I am given to understand that the present Duke of Argyll, the grandson of Elizabeth Gunning, has two other portraits of his ancestress, both half length, and that one of them is at his Grace's town residence at Campden-hill.

The "fair Gunnings" were painted as companion pictures by Cotes in 1751, and also by Read; the latter pictures were both engraved by Finlayson, and other engravings of Maria and Elizabeth are to be seen in the British Museum. Read represents the Duchess in a lace mob cap and cloak, while an engraving by Houston portrays her as a country lass, with a rose in her bosom. Of Maria there is a portrait by Hamilton, whole length, with a greyhound by her side. The two sisters are very much alike; both are remarkable for their small mouths, high foreheads, aquiline noses, and arched eyebrows. Certainly, Maria would be adjudged by the ladies nowadays the prettier in detail—she is slim and elegant. though rather inanimate; but I much prefer the looks of Elizabeth, who is darker, plumper, and more intelligent, and altogether a finer woman. I am told that there is also a mezzotint of "the three Miss Gunnings," but I have not been able to find a copy in the Print Room at the British Museum.

THE THELLUSSONS.

IT is stated as a fact, by a writer in the *Stock Exchange Review*, that "at the end of the last century, when George the Third was King, and when Meyer Anselm Rothschild kept a broker's shop in the Jew-lane of Frankfort, there were six bankers in London who had each and all the repute of being possessed of extraordinary wealth, or what would now be termed millionaires. These six bankers," he adds, "were Thomas Coutts, Francis Baring, Joseph Denison, Henry Hope, Lewis Tessier, and Peter Thellusson." I purpose in my present chapter to tell my readers a little about the latter wealthy gentleman, what sort of will he made, and what became of his wealth, which at one time threatened to prove of fabulous amount, to swallow up half the riches of his contemporaries, and to form the nucleus of a fortune which should fairly outstrip the Rothschilds and Esterhazys.

We are told by Sir Nathaniel William Wraxall, in his amusing "Memoirs of My own Time," that George the Third had a very great objection to raise to the peerage any member of a family engaged in commercial pursuits; and it was long before he could be persuaded—even by his favourite "heaven-born" minister, William Pitt —to break his resolution. The first to burst down the barrier of royal exclusiveness was Mr. Robert Smith, a banker in London, and the son of a banker at Nottingham, to whom Pitt was largely indebted for the "sinews of war" in the earlier part of his career, and on whom, therefore, was conferred, in 1797, the title of Lord Carrington, or, as the family now spell it, Carington.

Another of the wealthy money-changers and money-brokers, whose fortunes were established by successful commerce, east of Temple Bar, in the middle of the last century, was the aforesaid Peter Thellusson, who was born in 1735. Though not known to fame on this side the British Channel, yet, according to Sir Bernard Burke and the Heralds, the Thellussons trace back their origin to the *ancienne noblesse* of the kingdom of France. The first of the name of whom we hear anything in particular was Frederick de Thellusson, Seigneur de Fléschéres, and Baron de Saphorin, one among the nobles who assisted Philip VI. of France in his expedition into Flanders early in the fourteenth century. His family still owned their hereditary estates at Fléschéres, near Lyons, up to the time of the great Massacre of St. Bartholomew, in August, 1572, when they fell among the victims of that dreadful night. According to tradition, the only member of the family who escaped the slaughter was Theophilus de Thellusson, who had married a sister of the Count de Saluce, at that time the Governor of the city of Lyons; he seems to have effected his escape into Savoy, and thence to Geneva, where he settled, and his descendants at different times filled high places connected with the Republic of that city.

Isaac de Thellusson, who established himself as a banker in a good way of business in Geneva, and afterwards at Paris, and who was Ambassador from his native city to the Court of France in the reign of Louis XV., had four sons, one of whom, Peter, became the great merchant of London, whom we have already named. His history is certainly a very singular one. The father had largely increased his business by taking into his employ as a clerk, and afterwards as a partner, a man subsequently celebrated in French history, M. Necker, the same who was Minister of Finance during the French Revolution. The firm accordingly became known as Messrs. Thellusson and Necker. The son had joined his father's banking house in Paris when a young man; but as soon as the first throes of the Revolution made themselves felt, he resolved to seek a country where property would be more secure, and with that view to establish in London a branch in connection with his father's business. His great and absorbing passion seems to have been to acquire a large fortune in hard cash; and many years had not elapsed ere Mr. Peter Thellusson found his sails swelling with the breezes of favouring fortune, for he succeeded in establishing one of the principal banking houses in the City.

"A man of great sagacity and extraordinary perseverance," writes Mr. F. Martin, "coupled with a desire of making money, which amounted to an all-absorbing passion. Mr. Thellusson soon found success at his door, and in a few years built up one of the first banking establishments in the British metropolis." But however great his wealth, he still yearned for more. Accordingly unsated with the gold which he had accumulated, he resolved, as he knew that he could not live for ever himself, to try at least if he could not hand down a colossal fortune to his distant posterity, either entire or in three shares, he did not much care which. Probably such a will as he devised, in order to effect that end, had never been heard of, or even dreamt of, before the year of grace 1797; the sequel will prove that it is a good thing for society at large that there have not been many found to imitate his example; and it is well that, although his will was allowed to stand, the recurrence of such a disposition was forbidden by a special Act of Parliament.

Towards the close of the last century, when he was still several years short of the allotted "three score and ten," he one day quietly took stock of his worldly possessions, and found that he was the owner of a clear £6,000,000 in hard cash, besides an annual rent roll of £4,500. He "had satisfied the ordinary ambition of an English bourgeois—he had founded a family. Peter Isaac, the son of his youth and the prop of his house, was heir to £35,000 a year in money and land, and might claim to be a born gentleman. Peers and peeresses might hereafter spring in intermediate succession from the loins of that denizen of a dingy little back parlour behind the Bank. The best men upon 'Change envied the prosperous Peter Thellusson, who had no object of ambition unsatisfied. Peter himself was of a different mind; he had not nearly money enough. Let other men be content to found one family; Peter was lucky enough to have three sons, and he would found three families. It was not that he loved his sons, or his sons' sons; but it was the hope and desire of this magnificent posthumous miser to associate his name with three colossal fortunes. If he did not love his sons, he did not hate them; he was simply indifferent to everything except to his one cherished object."

Accordingly he took the very best legal advice upon the subject, and made, as most men make, a will. By this he left about £100,000 to his wife, his three sons, and three daughters —probably in order to show the world that no unnatural antipathy to his nearest relatives tainted his last dying testament with mania; while the rest of his fortune, amounting to more than £600,000, was conveyed to trustees, who were to let it accumulate till after the deaths not only of his children, but of all the male issue of his sons and grandsons; in fact, till every man, woman, and child of the offspring of Peter, and alive or begotten at Peter's decease, should be defunct. After that event the vast property, with its accumulations at compound interest, was to be given to the nearest male descendants who should bear the family name of Thellusson. No one of the children or grandchildren who had smiled in old Peter Thellusson's face, or had trembled at his presence, or had squalled at the sound of his hard, harsh voice, should be ever the better or richer for all his wealth. The money, divided into three equal parts, was to go to the eldest male descendants of his eldest, his second, and his third sons respectively. If there should be a failure in the male issue of any of the three, the share was to be divided among the representatives of the other two; if a failure of two, then the three shares were to go as one vast property to the one survivor; but, should after all no lineal male descendants then remain, the whole was directed to be sold, in order that it might be applied towards paying off a part of the national debt! This was the grandest part, perhaps, of all his scheme; the very idea of it is bewildering to the ordinary business mind.

Having done what he pleased with his own, and excluded, like an unnatural parent, his own offspring from almost any share in the benefit of the estate which he held in trust for " those of his own household," he winds up his testament with a whining appeal to the Legislature, almost worthy of Shylock appealing against mercy; he had earned his money by honest industry, and he humbly trusted that the two Houses of Parliament would not alter his will. But, though man proposes, a higher Power disposes; and this Mr. Thellusson's family learned speedily. With such intentions recorded in his will, which he duly signed and sealed, Peter Thellusson died; but those intentions, like so many others in this world, were doomed to be frustrated. The family met after the funeral and the will was opened, and created sensations which vibrated through the land in widening circles. Our law books picture to us the blank disappointment of the then living relatives, the gentle murmur of a past generation of lawyers, and the gaping wonder of the general public. There were then alive three sons and six grandsons of this malignant old merchant, " all destined to live the life of Tantalus; to see this great pagoda tree growing up before them, yet never to pluck one unit of its fruit." The terms of the will enjoined, that when the last survivor of all the nine children and grandchildren should yield up his breath, then the charm was to end; the great mountain of accumulated wealth was to be divided into three portions, and one-third was to be given to each of the " eldest male lineal descendant" of his three sons. It is indeed strange to think that so shrewd a man should have had apparently no suspicion that his nearest relations would do anything rather than rest content under such a will, or that the Court of Chancery under Lord Eldon would not engulph in its wide jaws a good portion of his fortune under such tempting conditions. And so it came to pass that in something less than two years after Peter Thellusson was gathered to his fathers, two bills had been filed in Chancery impeaching the will, the one by his widow and children, and the other by his trustees.

But although the suits were unsuccessful, the will being allowed to stand good by the Lord Chancellor and the other judges of the court, who decided in favour of the testator, yet, for years after, members of the bar found a rich mine which they were not unwilling to work in cases connected with the Thellusson will; and only a few years of the present century had elapsed when poor Mrs Thellusson, the widow, died—it is said of a broken heart.

To be brief, such men as Lords Loughborough, and Alvanley, and Eldon, allowed the litigation to go up to the House of Lords, by which the will was confirmed. The Legislature, however, afterwards took up the affair, and, although they would not set aside the will by an *ex post facto* law, they enacted that the power of devising property for the purpose of accumulation shall be restrained in general to twenty-one years after the death of the testator. It was calculated at the time that the Thellusson fund, if it had been left to accumulate as its founder had specified, could not have amounted to less than £19,000,000 at the moment of distribution, and would very probably have reached the figure of £32,000,000. But this calculation was rash. It was beautifully correct in theory and on paper, but would not work in practice; evidently, too, not a shadow of a doubt existed in his mind when he made the will, that by the simple process of allowing a large capital locked up under the protection of the law to accumulate through three generations, the wealth of the future Thellusson would swell into dimensions compared with which fortunes of kings and emperors would be mere beggarly flea-bites. Unfortunately for himself, he had left out of his calculation one all-important item, the existence of a certain institution called the Court of Chancery, with its array of long-robed worship, all ready to claim a share in the interest and compound interest. The Court of Chancery so " clipped and pollarded Peter Thellusson's oak that it was not much larger than when he left it."

Not only was there a Chancery suit to set aside the will, but there was a cross suit to have the trusts of the will performed under the direction of the Court of Chancery—a suit which at sixty years old was as lively as ever. Of, course, there were also other suits; suits about post-testament acquisitions, about advowsons, &c. The last survivor of the nine lives died in February, 1856.

The unhappy lady who was the wife of this selfish millionaire, was a Miss Woodford, the daughter of Mr Matthew Woodford, and sister of Sir Ralph Woodford, of Carlby, sometime M.P. for Evesham. She derived but little comfort from her husband's bank notes, and owned with her last breath that the source of true happiness is not to be looked for in money bags.

Seats in the House of Commons were found for all the three sons of Peter Thellusson; the Irish Barony of Rendlesham was conferred on the eldest, Peter Isaac, in 1806, and three of this nobleman's sons having held the title in succession, the latter now belongs to his grandson, the fifth Lord Rendlesham.

But the many millions sterling which the great merchant had hoped would eventually come to his descendants, what has become of them? The money was never destined to be theirs in its integrity; and but a comparatively modest fortune remained, and still remains, to the house. Lord Rendlesham, the head of the family, holds a seat in the House of Commons, as one of the Members for Suffolk, in which county he owns a fair estate; but though only eighty years have passed since old Peter Thellusson's death, there is now no banking house which bears his name in the great world of London. *Sic transit gloria mundi.*

THE NOBLE HOUSE OF CECIL.

IF HORACE WALPOLE was allowed to manufacture such a word as "Double-Duchessed" as an epithet to the fair Miss Gunning, who married successively the Dukes of Hamilton and Argyll, I suppose that I may be pardoned if I take a similar liberty and ask my readers to pardon me for giving them a brief account of the "Double-Marquissed" House of Cecil. It is not often that two members of the same family are created Earls in a single day, and that their respective male descendants attain a still higher step in the peerage after a lapse of nearly two centuries. Yet such is the history of the Cecils, now Earls and Marquises of Exeter and of Salisbury.

And first it may strike my readers as strange that, though the name of Cecil is no older than the reign of Queen Mary, yet the ancestors of this two-fold marquisate were a very ancient stock; for did not Robert Sisilt assist Robert Fitz-Hamon in the conquest of Glamorganshire and Gower Land, under William Rufus? And did he not receive, in recompense for his services, the fair manor oi Alterennes, in the County of Hereford? And was not his son and heir Sir James Sisilt, of Beaufort, in the County of Glamorgan? and did he not fall at the siege of Wallingford, "having then on him a vesture with his arms and ensigns in needlework, as they afterwards appeared on the tomb of his descendant, Gerard, in the Abbey of Dore,"—the same which were formally assigned by the King to his lineal descendant, Sir John Sisilt, and the same which are now borne by the Marquises of Exeter and of Salisbury, viz., "Barry of ten, arg. and az. over all six escutcheons, three, two, and one, sa.. each charged with a lion rampant of the first"— the latter, adds Sir Bernard Burke, "with a crescent for difference?" I pass over some seven or eight generations, and come to the above-named Sir John Sisilt, concerning whom Mr. Sharpe relates in his "Present Peerage" that a fierce contest arose at Halidon Hill in 1333 between him and Sir William de Fakenham respecting the arms thus heraldically described. On this occasion they were adjudged to Sir John by a commission from Edward III., who forbade the rival knights from meeting and doing battle for the shield in single and possibly in deadly combat. His great grandson Philip appears to have spelt his name as Sicelt, which was again modernised into Cyssel by his son David, Sergeant-at-Arms and steward of the manor of Weston, in Northamptonshire, memorable in after-time as the place where Henry VIII. parted with his daughter, the Lady Margaret, who eventually became the ancestress of the Stewart and Brunswick lines.

David's son, Richard, who appears to have called himself indifferently Sitcell, Sicelt, or Syssel, was page and groom of the wardrobe to "bluff King Hal" and Constable of Warwick Castle; and he attended Henry as one of his Court on his interview with Francis, King of France, on the Field of the Cloth of Gold. He is described as being "of Burley," and he certainly served as High Sheriff of Rutlandshire in 1539. He received from the Crown a grant of 300 acres in St. Martin's at Stamford, together with the site of St. Michael's Priory; and he seems also to have purchased the manor of Esyngdon, or Essendon, in Rutlandshire, whence his grandson, the first Lord Salisbury, took the title of Lord Cecil of Essendon.

This gentleman was the father of a statesman whose name is familiar to every reader of the History of England under the reigns of the Tudors and Stuarts—William, Lord Burghley. I will not, however, speak here of the great Burleigh in his capacity of a statesman, but only as a private individual. He was an ardent and zealous genealogist, when his public duties gave him time for such pursuits; and his labours or amusements in this direction, though they often related to other families than his own, were sometimes directed to researches into the early annals of his own house. An excessive eagerness for the credit of a noble ancestry was one of his foibles; and a leading antiquary of the day, taking advantage of the classical appearance of the newly-adapted name of Cecil, endeavoured to court his favour by gravely trying to trace his descent from a patrician house of ancient Rome—the *gens Cæcilia!*

Passing, however, from the realm of myth to that of plain prose and history, and coming to his early manhood, I find him at the age of twenty-one a student in Gray's Inn. Inclining strongly to the " new faith," he attracted King Henry's notice and favour by a successful disputation, which he held with two intemperate chaplains of O'Neill, the Irish chieftain, as to the limits of the power of the Roman Pontiff. The King accordingly granted him the reversion of the office of "custos brevium" in one of the courts of law; and his career henceforth forms part of English history. I will therefore dwell briefly on it, simply stating that, on the Protector Somerset establishing a Court of Requests in his own house, he appointed Sir William Cecil its first master. The latter subsequently followed his patron to Scotland, and on the field of Musselburgh he narrowly escaped death from a cannon ball which passed close beside him. On his return south he was made Secretary of State, and sworn a member of the Privy Council. On the fall of Somerset he was sent to the Tower to share his chief's imprisonment. Released thence, I find him restored to his high post, in which, says Sharpe, "Queen Mary offered to retain him permanently if he would consent to abjure the Protestant faith; this, however, he refused to do." The rest of his story shall be told in the words of Sir Bernard Burke, which differ slightly from the above statement:

"Under the rule of Mary, although a very zealous reformist previously, Sir William, with all the tact of that renowned churchman, the vicar of Bray, doffed his Protestant mantle, and conformed to the ancient faith—outwardly, says his biographer, Dr. Nares, but certainly so far as engaging a Catholic domestic chaplain, humbling himself at the confessional, and kneeling before the altar of the real presence, constitute such a confirmation. This outward demonstration proved not to have been assumed in vain, for we find the wily politician enjoying again the sunshine of royal favour, and actually nominated, with Lord Paget and Sir Edward Hastings, to conduct Cardinal Pole, then invested with a legatine commission, into England. In this reign Cecil represented the county of Lincoln in Parliament. Immediately upon the accession of Elizabeth, however, with whom he constantly corresponded, and on whose accession he was the first person of whom the new Queen sought advice, he became once more a staunch denouncer of Popish errors; the star of his fortune arose, and few statesmen have been guided through a more brilliant course. His first official employment was the resumption of the secretary-of-stateship, and in that post, so sensible was his royal mistress of his important services that she elevated him to the peerage, by the title of Baron Burghley, in 1571, although at this period his private fortune does not appear to have been much advanced; for by a letter written by himself just after his elevation he says that he is "the poorest lord in England." Soon after this, however, he obtained a post of more profit as well as honour, that of "Master of the Court of Wards," which he held along with his portfolio of State. A conspiracy was soon afterwards discovered against his life, and the two assassins, Barney and Natter, declared at their execution that they were instigated by the Spanish ambassador, for which, and other offences, his Excellency was ordered to depart the kingdom. As a consolation for these perils, the secretary was honoured with the Order of the Garter in June, 1572, and in the September following, at the decease of the Marquess of Winchester, was appointed Lord High Treasurer, and was Chancellor of the University of Cambridge for forty years, from 1558 to 1598."

His mode of living, say contemporary writers, was in keeping with his rank and the custom of the times. "He had four places of residence—his lodgings at Court, his house in the Strand, his family seat at Burleigh, and his own favourite seat of Theobalds," near Waltham Cross, to which he loved to retire from harness. At his house in London, he (when free) supported a family of fourscore persons, without counting those who attended him in public.

"He kept a standing table for gentlemen, and two other tables for those of a meaner condition," says Sir Bernard Burke; and these were always served alike, whether he was in or out of town. Twelve times he entertained Elizabeth at his house, on more than one occasion for some weeks together; and as Royal visits are rather expensive luxuries, and Elizabeth formed no exception to the rule, (for they cost each between £1000 and £2000,) the only wonder is that his purse was not exhausted, and that he was able to leave his son £25,000 in money and valuable effects, besides £4000 a year in landed estates. Be this, however, as it may, his son Thomas, who was raised to the earldom of Exeter in 1605, complained loudly of his poverty, which on one occasion he urged as an excuse for declining the honour of a step in the peerage, writing to the Attorney-General, in 1606, that "he was resolved to content himself with the estate (degree) which he had, of a baron, and that he found his estate little enough to maintain the degree he was in."

It is somewhat strange to add that two years later he and his younger brother, Robert, were both created earls, and on the very same day,

May 4, Lord Burghley taking the title of Exeter, and his brother that of Salisbury. It is still more strange that the younger brother on this occasion should have taken precedence of the elder, his patent having passed the Great Seal in the morning, while that of Lord Burghley, it is said, did not take effect till the afternoon or evening. This accident is reported to have occasioned some ill blood between the brothers at the time, though they were soon reconciled by finding themselves obliged to make common cause against the satirists of the age, who were not slow to attack the twin earls of yesterday, as mere courtiers and place-hunters, and men of no great family pretensions.

On this subject the old Lord High Treasurer had always been most tenacious; and his sons, it would seem, followed his example. At all events, in the Harleian MSS. I find the following curious letter from Lord Exeter, evidently written at this time, which is well worth giving here at length, on account of its bearing on the mooted question of the difference between a "Gentleman" and an "Esquire."

"There is some cause of late fallen out of one that gives reproachful words to my brother, and therewithal said that it was a strange thing that such a one as he, whose grandfather was a sieve-maker, should rule the whole state of England; and though the malice of the party was towards him, yet I must be likewise sensible thereof myself, both being descended from him; therefore I have thought good to require you forthwith to take the pains to make search in my study at Burghley, amongst my boxes, of my evidences, and I think you will find the very writ itself by which my grandfather or great-grandfather, or both, were made sheriffs of Lincolnshire or Northamptonshire, and likewise a warrant from the Duke of Suffolk, in King Henry VIII.'s time, to my grandfather and old Mr. Wingfield, that dead is, for the certifying touching the fall of woods in Clyff Park or Rockingham Forest, by the name of David Cecyle *Esquire;* which title at those days was not used but to such that were gentlemen of note, where commonly they were entitled but by the name of *gentlemen*. If you have any record of your own to show the descent of my great-grandfather, I pray you send a note thereof likewise. My lord, my father's altering the writing of his name maketh many that are not very well affected to our house to doubt whether we be rightly descended from the house of Wales, because they write their names 'Sitsilt,' and our name is written 'Cecyle;' my grandfather wrote it 'Syssell;' and so in orthography all these names differ, whereof I marvel what moved my lord my father to alter it. I have my lord's pedigree very well set out, which he left unto me. I pray you let this be secret unto yourself, which my brother of Salisbury desired me so to give in charge unto you; and so I commend you very kindly unto yourself and my good aunt, your wife; from London, this 13th of November, 1605.

"Your very loving cousin and friend,
"EXETER.

"To Hugh Allington, Esquire."

Lord Exeter, who always maintained an unblemished character among statesmen who were not all free from blemish, was certainly a man of high talents and good sense; and he did well in contenting himself with the reflected dignity of his father's splendid name, and in leaving it to his brother to emulate it in the exercise of the higher offices of statecraft.

Robert, the younger brother, the Earl of Salisbury, though successively Secretary of State and Lord High Treasurer—as his father had been before him—married a sister of the unhappy Henry Brooke, Lord Cobham, and died, worn out with the cares of public office and political life, within six years after gaining his coronet. In his last illness he was heard to say to Sir Walter Cope, "Ease and pleasure quake to hear of death; but my life, full of cares and miseries, desireth to be dissolved." He had some years previously addressed a letter to Sir James Harrington, the poet, in pretty much the same tone. "Good knight," saith the minister, "rest content, and give heed to one that hath sorrowed in the bright lustre of a court, and gone heavily on even the best-seeming fair ground. 'Tis a great task to prove one's honesty and yet not mar one's fortune. You have tasted a little thereof in our good queen's time, who was more than a man, and, in truth, sometimes less than a woman. I wish I waited now in your presence-chamber, with ease at my food and rest in my bed. I am pushed from the shore of comfort, and know not where the winds and waves of a court will bear me. I know it bringing little comfort on earth; and he is, I reckon, no wise man that looketh this way to heaven."

His son and successor continued the younger line of the Cecils as Earls of Salisbury through six generations, when James, the seventh earl, was raised in 1789 to the Marquisate by George III., on the recommendation of Mr. Pitt. The grandson of this nobleman (I may remark by way of parenthesis) is the present Marquis of Salisbury, who held high office under the Conservative administration of Lord Derby, and is now Chancellor of the University of Oxford. But to return. Twelve years more were destined to elapse before the like honour of a marquis's coronet was extended to the elder branch of the Cecils, of Burleigh, and of Exeter. Around this elder house, however, there is a great halo of romance.

I have already acquainted my readers that the two sons of the great Lord Burleigh were raised in one day by James I., to the earldoms of Salisbury and Exeter, and that in 1789 the younger line, that of Salisbury, exchanged an earl's coronet for that of a marquis. The same good fortune befell the head of the elder house in 1801, when Henry, tenth Earl of Exeter and eleventh Lord Burleigh, was advanced one step in the peerage of the United Kingdom, by the favour of George III. and Mr. Pitt, by the "name, style, and title" of Marquis of Exeter. There is really not much to say about the intermediate earls, except that they were severally born, succeeded to the family coronet and pew in church, married, begot children, died, and "slept with their fathers." But the case was far different with Earl Henry, who, probably without ever intending or even dreaming of such a thing, suddenly found himself the hero of a romance of real life, or rather the actor of the protagonist's part in a drama of rural and peasant existence.

Born in the year 1754, the only son, and, indeed, the only child, of the Hon. Thomas Chambers Cecil, by his marriage with Miss Charlotte Gardner, Henry Cecil, at the age of nineteen, found himself at once an orphan and presumptive heir to the titles and estates of an old uncle who did not care for him a rush, and towards whom probably he felt very little affection or regard. At all events, no love was lost between them; so while the old earl lived the young man kept pretty clear of Burleigh and all its belongings, and travelled through various parts of England, rather enjoying a life of quiet and homely adventure than otherwise. He did not join the gipsies, as did Bampfylde Moore Carew; nor did he elope with an actress or some foreign duchess, as many young men would have done had they been left their own masters at an equally early age, and been known to have good pecuniary prospects. On the contrary, he married, quietly and soberly, into a good county family of the west of England, choosing as his bride the pretty Miss Vernon, only child of the squire of Hanbury Hall, in

Worcestershire. But the young lady did not answer his expectations; and in June, 1791, when he was just seven and thirty, he petitioned for and obtained a divorce. This judgment made him again a free man; and he resolved, having been once "taken in and done for," to look about for a second wife at his leisure, and to choose no one of whom he was not sure that he could mould her to his own tastes and ways, and that he would find in her a pattern of conjugal affection and domestic virtue. "Courts, and courtiers, and coronets," he would say, at all events to himself, "are all very well in their way; but their way is not my way; and, if I can only find a plain, homely, and truly virtuous maiden, in whatever sphere of life I discover her, in hall, in manor-house, in parsonage, or in cottage, then I swear with King Cophetua,

"This beggar-maid shall be my queen."

How far he was true to his oath the sequel will serve to show. I must ask my readers to accompany me—mentally of course—to a charming country village in Shropshire, nestling among green lanes and fruitful apple orchards, and called Bolas Magna; it is not far from Wellington and Newport, and within six or seven miles of that well-known inland beacon, the Wrekin.

It was a fine evening in the month of July, 1791, when the grass had been all mown and the hay had been made, and when the harvest had not commenced, that a stranger, apparently between thirty and forty years of age, stopped at the gate of a small farmer and shopkeeper in the village of Bolas. It was by no means a very usual thing to see a stranger in so retired a place, and at first the good man and his wife, who stood at the door, were inclined to refuse the hospitality which he asked. He certainly looked like a gentleman, at all events like a decent person; but what could a gentleman or any person be doing, wandering about a strange village, five miles at least from the nearest town, at such an hour? In spite of the evident suspicion of his *bona fides*, which was entertained by both of the old folks, the stranger urgently yet courteously pressed his demands, begging that at least he might be allowed to stay in their cottage till morning, even if he had only a chair to "rest upon in their lower room." He did not require a bed; but it was clear that a heavy thunderstorm was coming on, and surely they would not force him to go on his way in the midst of the rain and storm. At last the boon was granted, though it must be owned somewhat grudgingly; and next morning the guest who had thus forced himself upon them in their little "castle" made the formal acquaintance of honest Thomas Hoggins and his wife. Ah! it is not only in the olden time, or only in the regions of the distant East, that "strangers have entertained angels unawares." The stranger's pleasure in the society of Mr and Mrs Hoggins no doubt was enhanced by the appearance at the breakfast table of their daughter, Sarah, a rustic beauty of seventeen, a distant sight of whom on the previous evening, as she washed up "the things" in the kitchen, had fairly enchained his eyes and his heart. The adventure of an hour, connected with crooked roads and coming night, was about suddenly to affect the wanderer's future life, and still more so that of the village maiden who alternately sat beside him and waited on her parents and their unknown guest.

Breakfast was over; but from that humble cottage where he had slept in a chair in the parlour, from those fields where Sarah Hoggins milked the cows, and from that dairy where her fair hands churned the cream into butter, Mr. Jones—for so the stranger styled himself—could not be persuaded to stir. He was a puzzle and a mystery; and there was no Œdipus at hand to solve the riddle of his being—who he was and where he came from. In answer to all inquiries, he spoke vaguely and unsatisfactorily; at last he said he was an "undertaker," or something of the kind, taking refuge in the vagueness of the term. Possibly such a vocation might serve to account for the air of tender melancholy which seemed to surround him; or possibly the word might have been meant as a gentle hint to Sarah Hoggins that, stranger as he was, he was ready to undertake any office, however new to him or he to it, in which she herself bore a part. Tennyson, who has made the story which I am about to tell familiar to most English readers, true to the poetic art, makes him out as calling himself not an "undertaker" but a "landscape painter."

A week or two passed, and by the arrival of harvest time the presence of Mr. Jones in the village had already become a fixed idea. The inhabitants looked upon him with a respectful fear. As weeks went on he made occasional absences from Bolas; these were always short, and confined to two or three days; and on his return he seemed to abound with money. The natives of Salop are not dull. They put the money and the absences together, and they whispered the result to one another. They felt sure Jones was a highwayman, and possibly the tortuous and tree-darkened lanes, and the stories of highwaymen and footpads on the roads around Bolas Magna may have made the robber idea unpleasantly credible. Probably they did not reflect that such a sparse country, so rarely visited by strangers, would not support a single footpad unless he possessed a large capital and could afford to abide the event.

After awhile, Mr. Jones, or Mr. Cecil—we may as well drop the *alias*—became the avowed suitor of Sarah Hoggins; but the notion that he was a highwayman still clung to her mother's mind, and she sturdily set her face against the connection. The father's logic was simple, and ultimately prevailed: " Why, my dear, he has plenty of money."

He showed his easy circumstances, indeed, by taking land, and by buying a site, on which he erected the largest house in the neighbourhood, now called Burleigh Villa. It stands amongst fields, facing the Wrekin, some seven miles distant from that landmark.

The wooing and the love-making of Mr. Cecil was brief; for on the 3rd of October, just as harvest was over, and the orchards were being stripped of the apples for cider, he and Sarah Hoggins were married in the little church of Bolas. But still who Henry Cecil was, and what was his parentage, remained a mystery to all, even to Sarah herself. They still continued to live on in the village—it is said in the old folk's house. Next year a little daughter was born to them, but died when only a few days old. She was buried in the little churchyard; but the grave is now forgotten.

A little more than two years passed by, and. in spite of the mystery which surrounded him, the respectability of Mr. Cecil's manners and conduct began to inspire the villagers of Bolas with confidence, so that they even appointed him to a post of trust as overseer, or churchwarden, or parish-constable. During this time, he was careful to supply by education all the accomplishments which might be supposed to be wanting in a peasant girl, who had become a wife and a mother.

He was thus circumstanced, when towards the end of December, 1793, when he had been married a little over two years, he read in a country paper the tidings of the death of his uncle, the old earl. His presence, he knew, would now be required at Burghley:

"Burghley House by Stamford Town."

and though it was the depth of winter, he resolved to travel thither, taking his wife with him, and to give her an agreeable surprise.

From Bolas, accordingly, one fine morning in January, having said goodbye to Mr. and Mrs. Hoggins, Henry Cecil and his wife, now just nineteen years of age, set out on horseback for a destination of which she was ignorant. Her husband merely told her that he was called on business into Lincolnshire, and that she must accompany him. Like a good and trustful wife, she at once obeyed his wish, and made the journey seated, as was the fashion of the day, on a pillion behind him. They rode on through Cannock Chase, past Lichfield and Leicester, stopping at various gentlemen's and noblemen's seats on the road, till at last they came within sight of a noble Elizabethan mansion situated in a lordly park.

Sarah Cecil gazed in admiration, and quietly remarked, "What a magnificent house!"

"How should you like, my dear Sally, to be mistress of such a place?" was her lord's reply.

"Very much indeed, if we were rich enough to live in it."

"I am glad that you like it; the place is yours. I am Earl of Exeter, and you are not plain Mrs. Cecil, but my Countess."

She could scarcely believe her ears; but she could not mistrust the fond and honest words of her husband. The mystery of the last two years was solved at last—to her at least. Mr. Cecil was no highwayman, that she knew already; but a painter of landscapes he might be. It was, however, indeed strange news to her that he was one of the proud peers of England, and that she had the coronet of a countess for her own. In a few minutes they reached the great entrance; and there was a fresh trial for her nerves, as a crowd of powdered servants came forward to recognise their new lord and master, who lost no time in presenting to them their future mistress.

This journey has been immortalised by Tennyson in his ballad of "The Lord of Burleigh:"

> "Thus her heart rejoiceth greatly,
>   Till a gateway she discerns,
> With armorial bearings stately,
>   And beneath the gate she turns;
>
> "Sees a mansion more majestic
>   Than all those she saw before;
> Many a gallant gay domestic
>   Bows before him at the door;
>
> "And they speak in gentle murmur
>   When they answer to his call,
> While he treads with footstep firmer
>   Leading on from hall to hall.
>
> "And while now she wonders blindly,
>   Nor the meaning can divine,
> Proudly turns he round and kindly,
>   'All of that is mine and thine.'

> "Here he lives in state and bounty
> Lord of Burleigh fair and free,
> Not a lord in all the county
> Is so great a lord as he."

The news of the romantic story spread like wildfire throughout the neighbourhood, and the curiosity of the three counties of Lincoln, Rutland, and Northampton, which all meet within a few miles of Burleigh, was soon gratified by witnessing the entry of the peasant girl of Bolas upon the new sphere of life to which providence had raised her without her own seeking.

The happiness of the Earl and his Countess was unalloyed: she did ample justice to his choice, and became the partner of his joys and of his sorrows. But their married life was brief. Besides their first-born, who lies buried at Bolas, Sarah Hoggins had three children—a daughter and two sons. The younger son, Lord Thomas Cecil (after giving birth to whom she died in childbed) lived till 1873; the elder son inherited his father's earldom, and also the marquisate conferred on him in 1801, as already stated; the daughter married the late Right Hon. Henry Manvers Pierrepont, by whom she was the mother of Lady Charles Wellesley, who is again the mother of the heir to the honours of the house of Wellesley. Thus strangely enough the future

Duke of Wellington is the great-grandson of the peasant girl, who in 1791 milked cows and churned cream in the village of Bolas Magna.

A friend of mine, who a few years ago travelled in Shropshire, sent me at the time so graphic a description of a pilgrimage which he then made to the scene of this romance, that I venture to give part of it in his own words to my readers:

"Whilst on a visit, a fortnight since, in Shropshire, in sight of that cynosure of neighbouring eyes, the Wrekin, I found myself near the scene of one of the most romantic pages in the history of the English Peerage. On a pleasant September afternoon, when the sunlight was bathing the broad pastures, tinging the apples and damsons on the heavily-laden trees, and falling ruddy on the sides of red stone quarries, I bent my steps in the direction of the little village of Bolas Magna—not without some misgivings of losing my way among the little-frequented country roads which lead thither. But a story that Moore has sung, and which has furnished Tennyson with the subject of one of his best poems, was inducement enough to make me strive against my terrible want of topographical acumen, to pace the very spot so consecrate to love, and, if possible, converse with the remaining few who still recall persons and events dating more than seventy years ago.

After telling the story, much as I have told it to my readers, my friend proceeds:

"My walk led me past Burleigh Villa. It is a substantial brick house, the front diversified by two bays; and attached to it are good offices and farm buildings. A wealthy farmer now occupies it; and, as if still to connect the tradition of Cupid and Hymen's doings with the house, its master, the morning I paid my visit to the spot, had led a third bride to the saffron-coloured altar. Crossing the little river Muse, I entered the village of Great Bolas. It is the *beau idéal* of an English hamlet—clean, picturesque, not fine, and with no excitement about it. There are hundreds like it scattered through our land. The houses, and they are few, are thatched, and irregularly placed. I entered one, which possessed a spacious lower room, beautifully neat and comfortable. Like many Shropshire houses, it had a fire burning under a boiler to prepare turnips for the cattle. Joining the cottage garden was a churchyard. The church is a small, uninteresting structure of red stone, but which, from its colour, at a little distance harmonises well with a clump of trees standing close to it. On the ground, which falls away rather steeply from the northern wall of the inclosure, stood Hoggins' farm, of which the only memorials remaining are a wicket by which it was approached, and a well. The old man whose house I entered was parish clerk. Even he had forgotten the grave of the first-born child; but he was well acquainted with the circumstances of this story. His wife, who was ill in bed, recollected the persons of Mr. and Mrs. Cecil. Unable to converse with this link between the past and the present, I was more fortunate, in walking from the village, to meet an aged woman, her chin adorned with a grey beard, whose memory retained not only the action, but the persons of the drama.

"The picture of the 'Peasant Countess,' in the billiard-room at Burghley House, represents her as beautiful: the pencil of Lawrence would hardly do less for so interesting a sitter; but my inquiries as to her beauty raised no enthusiastic response. The old woman would not even admit that she was handsome. 'She might have been well-looking,' was the extent of her praise. A male informant told me he believed Sarah Hoggins was a 'straight lass.' Shade of Hogarth! What a description of beauty!"

The poet has beautifully described the drooping of a flower removed from its native air into a higher level. He has said that the village maiden received with extreme grace the homage and love of those about her; yet that her heart was being eaten out by yearnings for the little village and the old farm, and the simple faces of those among whom she lived in the days of her youth. These influences may have contributed somewhat towards her early death; but the mediate cause took effect in childbirth, and happened only a very few years after she had arrived at her honours, at the early age of twenty-four.

> "And a gentle consort made he,
>   And her gentle mind was such
> That she grew a noble lady,
>   And the people lov'd her much.
>
> "But a trouble weigh'd upon her
>   And perplex'd her night and morn,
> With the burden of an honour
>   Unto which she was not born.
>
> "Faint she grew and ever fainter,
>   And she murmured, 'Oh, that he
> Were once more that landscape painter
>   Which did win my heart from me.'
>
> "So she droop'd and droop'd before him,
>   Fading slowly from his side;
> Three fair children first she bore him,
>   Then before her time she died."

The school of Werther is not a numerous school among our English nobility, whether titled or untitled; but even at the time of Mr.

Henry Cecil's love adventure, the spirit of romanticism had penetrated the French and German nations, and also, to some extent, the English. But whether it was the cause or the effect of that revolutionary earthquake which eighty years since was rocking the people of Europe, at all events it had subsided along with those wild political enthusiasms which stirred many fine souls to their lowest depths. For the most part, the alliances of "the Upper Ten Thousand" nowadays are made upon considerations which effectually shut out all chance of a rustic love, however real and genuine, ending in matrimony. Nevertheless, from the day when King Cophetua wedded the "beggar-maide" down to the present hour, a few sporadic cases have occurred in high circles in which love, as a kind of eccentricity, I suppose, has broken through the cold and calculating rules which prevail under our social code. And yet, who can say how much benefit some noble families have gained by the transfusion into their veins of a little admixture of plebeian blood, red with country health and free from the taint of courts and cities?

The romantic tale of Sarah Hoggins, with only a few variations, has also been popularized in another way, namely, as an oratorio, which has been performed with much success at more than one Musical Festival—for instance at Birmingham in 1875, when it achieved a great success. It was thus described at the time:

"The story illustrated in music by the composer, Signor Schira, is a pleasing and graceful one, and the music makes an admirable match to the words. The subject is essentially pastoral and fanciful, a theme which novelists and poets in all ages have loved to tell, in both simple prose and in ambitious verse. A powerful lord, 'the Lord of Burleigh,' in one of his wanderings in quest of subjects to fill his sketch-book, under the modest title of his Christian name, has wooed and won the affections of a simple rustic beauty, named Marian. On the conclusion of the marriage festivities the artist-nobleman and his bride set out, professedly to seek their fortunes, accompanied only by Marian's old playmate, Constance. On their journey they turn aside, led seemingly by an idle impulse, to survey a lordly mansion, near which the road passes, when, to the amazement of Marian, her husband conducts her through the gates, not only without opposition, but with every mark of respect and welcome from the attendants. Cecil then flings off his disguise and avows his stratagem, secure in the conviction that Marian loves him for himself alone; but the burden of the state to which she is so suddenly lifted weighs heavily upon his rustic bride, and the happiness of the lovers is shortly ended by the decline and death of Marian,

> "Who, like a lily drooping,
> Bows down her head and dies."

A termination sad enough to satisfy the most ardent lovers of the 'tear-compelling ballad,' and sufficiently suggestive of variety to give the utmost charm when set to characteristic music; and as Signor Schira approached his task in the spirit of both poet and musician, the successful result already spoken of was a matter for little surprise. The character of the music is so happy in form and treatment that the mind is put to no effort to conjure up the several scenes as the music progresses. Now we can see the bridal procession winding down the green hill to the valley in which the moss-covered village church stands, grey with age, the bride and bridegroom, truly 'a comely couple,' answering with glowing eyes the kind greetings on all sides, and then the quaint old mansion, bearing evidence of strength needed in a former time, when every lord's house was of necessity his castle, the wondering wife passing through lines of obsequious servants, and marvelling at the vast amount of respect with which she and her painter lover are welcomed; then the effects of transplanting the lovely flower of the field into the richer parterre of the garden; the sickness and death of Marian follow with a sad swiftness, making the story like an April day—

> "'Begun with a smile,
> To end with a sigh.'"

LAURENCE, EARL FERRERS.

AMONG the noblest and the proudest of our old English families deservedly stand the Shirleys, of Shirley in Derbyshire; of Staunton Harold, in Leicestershire; of Chartley, in Staffordshire; of Eatington, in Warwickshire; and of half a dozen other places, which are enumerated in the "Landed Gentry" of Sir Bernard Burke, who assigns to them an unbroken descent from the Anglo-Saxon days. And with good reason too; for does not that learned antiquary Sir Wm. Dugdale himself say that, "the name of their ancestor, Sewallis de Etingdon, argues him to have been of the old English stock?" The fact is that the lordship of Etingdon, or (as it is now termed) Eatington or Etington, was granted by William the Conqueror to one of his Norman followers, who appears to have left Sewallis in peaceful possession of his lands, though doubtless in nominal dependence on himself. In the course of years, possibly the Norman lords being absentees, and not looking well to their own interests, the descendants of Sewallis contrived to make good their hold, and to play first fiddle instead of second. At all events, at a very early date under our Norman sovereigns, the acknowledged lords of Eatington were Shirleys; and Mr. Sewallis Shirley, the younger, of Eatington, is at present one of the representatives of Warwickshire in Parliament, as his father and grandfather were before him.

Sir Ralph de Shirley held the manor of Eatington, and was also member for Warwickshire in the reign of Edward I., and his descendants, the lords of Eatington, took an active part in the Wars of the Roses and with France; and if any of my readers desire to know more on the subject, they will find ample information anent the family in three distinct MS. histories of the House of Shirley in the British Museum.

In the eighteenth generation from the above-named Saxon thane—as Dugdale styles him—I come to Sir Robert Shirley, a gallant knight and Privy Councillor in the time of William and Mary, who, having inherited the ancient barony of Ferrers de Chartley, in right of his mother,

Dorothy, daughter and heiress of Robert Devereux, Earl of Essex, the unfortunate favourite of Elizabeth, was raised in 1711 to the Earldom of Ferrers, and whose shield was destined to receive a melancholy tarnish in the person of one of his grandsons, whose story I come to tell.

The first Earl's eldest son dying without leaving issue male, the title passed to his second son, Henry, and as he died unmarried, it devolved in due course on Laurence Shirley, eldest son of his third son, the Hon. Laurence Shirley, by his wife Anne, daughter of Sir Walter Clarges, Bart.— probably one of the family after whom Clarges-street, Piccadilly, is named. Even as a boy it is recorded of him that he was of a moody and passionate temper, and that at times he had but little control over his words or his deeds. His uncle, whose death placed the coronet on his head, had been in confinement under a statute of lunacy, and after a short return of reason relapsed into a state of incurable madness, which ended only with his life. One of his aunts, too—the Lady Barbara Shirley—was confined as a lunatic. The young lord himself was so far a sharer in the hereditary disorder of his family as to be subject, even after he grew to manhood, to sudden, causeless, and outrageous passions. According to a writer in the *Gentleman's Magazine,* he would walk hastily about the room, clenching his fists, grinning, biting his lips, and talking to himself without having anything to ruffle his temper, and without being under the influence of liquor. He would also talk to himself incoherently for hours and hours after he had gone to bed. Nor was this all; he would entertain all sorts of groundless delusions and suspicions of those round about him; he would go about secretly armed with a dagger or a brace of pistols; when spoken to he was absent, and often would not reply; he would make odd mouths before a looking-glass, and spit upon it, and use all sorts of strange gestures, as if he was bewitched. It appears, too, that he had contracted a habit of drinking strong liquors while making what was then called the "Grand Tour," without which no member of "the quality" was considered to have finished his education.

In 1752 the eccentric nobleman had married a daughter of Sir William Meredith; but, though she was of a mild and gentle disposition, he treated her with great brutality. Nor was his wife the only member of his family to whom he so behaved himself. He was on ill terms with almost all his relations, and appears to have been a nuisance to the neighbourhood and to himself. One day when his brother William, a clergyman, got up from the table, not choosing to

sit longer over the bottle, and joined the ladies in
the drawing room, he followed him, and, standing
with his back to the fire, broke out into a violent
rage and insulted him in the presence of the company, though there was not a shadow of pretext
for any such treatment. The fact was that his
hereditary tendency to insanity had been fostered
and cherished by a fond and foolish mamma, who
had allowed the dear boy to have his own way in
everything when a child, and would not permit
his father to correct him. His temper had not
been improved by a legal separation which his
wife had lately obtained from him by an Act of
Parliament, which had also authorised the appointment of a person to receive the income of his
estates, and to control his expenditure. So
eccentric indeed, had he become that his family
solicitor, a Mr Goostrey, declined any longer to act
for him, and that, on account of an absurd and
groundless quarrel which he contrived to pick
with Sir Thomas Stapleton when staying in Lord
Westmoreland's house, his relatives had held a
cabinet council to discuss the question of applying for a commission of lunacy to be issued
against him. From this step, however, it appears
that they were deterred by the fact that he
enjoyed long intervals of sanity, and that if they
should fail they would be in danger of being sen-

tenced to pay a heavy fine as guilty of *scandalum magnatum*.

It appears too that about this period he took up his abode in lodgings at Muswell Hill, near Highgate and Hornsey, where he kept all sort of low company, whom he amused, no doubt, by his vulgar and eccentric conduct. He would drink coffee out of the spout of a kettle, mix his beer and porter with mud, and shave one side of his face only. He threatened on more than one occasion to "do for" his landlady upon the most trifling provocation in the world; and on one occasion he violently broke open on a Sunday a stable where his horse was locked up, knocking down with his fist the ostler's wife when she asked him to wait a few minutes while her husband brought the key. During this time, however, he managed his own affairs with shrewdness and penetration, so that Mr. Goostrey said it would be easier to cheat anyone in the county than the Earl, and that he was as sharp as any member of either House of Parliament in dealing with such a matter as the cutting off of an entail.

Mr. Cradock, in his "Literary and Miscellaneous Memoirs," speak of his Lordship as all but a madman. He writes:

"I still retain a strong impression of the unfortunate Earl Ferrers, who, with the Ladies

Shirley, his sisters, frequented Leicester races, and visited at my father's house. During the early part of the day, his lordship preserved the character of a polite scholar and a courteous nobleman, but in the evening he became the terror of the inhabitants; and I distinctly remember running up-stairs to hide myself, when an alarm was given that Lord Ferrers was coming armed, with a great mob after him. He had behaved well at the ordinary; the races were then in the afternoon, and the ladies regularly attended the balls. My father's house was situated midway between Lord Ferrers's lodgings and the town-hall, where the race assemblies were then held: he had, as was supposed, obtained liquor privately, and then became outrageous; for from our house he suddenly escaped and proceeded to the town-hall, and, after many most violent acts, threw a large silver tankard of scalding negus amongst the ladies; he was then secured for that evening. This was the last time of his appearing at Leicester, till brought from Ashby-de-la-Zouch to prison there. It has been much regretted by his friends that, as Lady Ferrers and some of his property had been taken from him, no greater precaution had been used with respect to his own safety, as well as that of all around him. Whilst sober, my father, who had a real regard for him, always urged that he was quite manageable; and when his sisters ventured to come with him to the races, they had an absolute reliance on his good intentions and promises."

Such was the character of Laurence, third Earl Ferrers, in the early part of the year 1760, when the tragic events which I am about to record took place. When it was ordered by the Court of Chancery that the rents due to Lord Ferrers should be paid to a receiver, the nomination of the said receiver was left to his lordship, who of course hoped to find in that person a pliant tool, who would take things easily, and let him have his own way. The person whom he so appointed was a Mr. John Johnson, his own steward, who had been in the service of the Shirleys for many years—even from boyhood. But he soon found out that Johnson would not oblige him at the expense of his honesty and his duty; and accordingly from that time he conceived an inveterate hatred towards him on account of the opposition which he offered to his crotchets. He never spoke of him except in terms of abuse and resentment, not to say with savage oaths; vowing that he had conspired with his enemies to do him a mortal injury, and was a villain, a scoundrel, and so forth. Further, he gave him warning to quit a farm of which he had long been tenant, and of which the trustees of the Ferrers estates had recently renewed the lease. But in this matter he could not get his own way, and from that time he resolved to move heaven and earth to obtain his revenge, even though he should have to " bide his time." He dissembled his feelings, however, so cleverly, that poor Johnson was led to believe that he never stood on better terms with the Earl, who all the while was meditating how to get rid of him.

In January, 1760, Lord Ferrers was at his seat of Staunton Harold, about two miles from Ashby-de-la-Zouch. His household consisted of a Mrs. C——, who lived with him nominally as his housekeeper, her four daughters, and five domestic servants—three maids, a boy, and an old man. Mr. Johnson's farmhouse, The Mount, was about a mile off across the park. On Sunday, the 18th of that month, Lord Ferrers called on Mr. Johnson, and, after some discourse, desired that he would come to him at Staunton on the following Friday at three o'clock in the afternoon. The Friday came round; and Johnson was true to his appointment. His lordship's dinner hour—like that of most country gentlemen of the time—was two o'clock; and rising early from table, shortly before the appointed hour, he desired Mrs. C—— to take the children for a walk, arranging that they were to return at five or half-past five o'clock, as the evenings were dark. The two men-servants also he contrived to get out of the way on different pretexts; so that when Mr. Johnson arrived there was no one in the house except the maids.

Three o'clock struck; punctual to his promise, Mr. Johnson knocked and rang the bell, and was ushered by the parlour-maid, Elizabeth Burland, into his lordship's private sitting-room. They had sat together talking on various matters for some ten minutes or more, when the Earl got up, walked to the door, and locked it. He next desired Johnson at once to settle some disputed account; then, rising higher in his demands, ordered him, as he valued his life, to sign a paper which he had drawn up, and which was a confession of his (Johnson's) villainy. Johnson expostulated and refused, as an honest man would refuse, to sign his name to any such document. The Earl then drew from his pocket a loaded pistol, and bade him kneel down, for that his last hour was come. Johnson bent one knee, but the Earl insisted on his kneeling on both his knees. He did so, and Lord Ferrers at once fired. The ball entered his body below the rib, but it did not do its fell work instantaneously. Though mortally wounded, the poor fellow had strength to rise, and to call loudly for assistance. The Earl at first coolly prepared as though he would discharge the other pistol, so as to put his victim out of misery; but, suddenly moved with remorse, he unlocked the door and called for the servants, who on hearing the discharge of the pistol had run in fear and trembling to the washhouse, not knowing whether his lordship would not take it into his head to send a bullet through their bodies also. He called them once and again, desired one to fetch a surgeon, and another to help the wounded man into a bed. It was clear, however, that Johnson had not many hours to live; and as he desired to see his children before he died, the Earl ordered that they should be summoned from the farm. Miss Johnson came speedily, and found her father apparently in the agonies of death, and Lord Ferrers standing by the bedside, and attempting to staunch the blood that flowed from the wound.

The whole neighbourhood was soon aroused, for the messenger who was sent for the doctor told the sad story to his friends and acquaintances along the road to Ashby, and by the time that the surgeon arrived there was a large crowd gathering round the house. His lordship now began to quake for his own life, and repeatedly implored the doctor not to allow him to be seized, declaring at the same time that he would shoot anyone who attempted to lay hands on him.

Fortunately, in order to deaden his feelings, his lordship had recourse to the porter jugs, which he continued to drain one after another, till he was hopelessly drunk; and for a few minutes he threatened to renew the attack on poor Johnson, whom he reviled and cursed as a villain, vowing that he would shoot him through the head as he lay in the bed. Soon, however, the paroxysm passed away; and at the end of the day, while his victim was still writhing in agony, his lordship, stupefied with drink, lay down to sleep.

During the night, by a clever *ruse*, the surgeon, Mr. Kirkland, contrived to have Johnson removed to his home in a sort of sedan chair which he extemporised for the occasion; but he survived the removal only a few hours, dying at nine o'clock the next morning.

The next part of the story shall be told in the words of the contemporary account as they stand in the *Gentleman's Magazine*.

"As soon as it became known that Mr. Johnson was really dead, the neighbours set about seizing the murderer. A few persons armed set out for Staunton, and as they entered the hall-yard they saw the Earl going towards the stable, as they imagined to take horse. He appeared to be just out of bed, his stockings being down and his garters in his hand, having probably taken the alarm immediately on coming out of his room and finding that Johnson had been removed. One Springthorpe, advancing towards his lordship presented a pistol, and required him to surrender; but his lordship putting his hand to his pocket, Springthorpe imagined he was feeling for a pistol, and stopped short, being probably intimidated. He thus suffered the Earl to escape back into the house, where he fastened the doors, and stood on his defence. The crowd of people who had come to apprehend him beset the house, and their number increased very fast. In about two hours Lord Ferrers appeared at the garret window, and called out, 'How is Johnson?' Springthorpe answered 'He is dead;' upon which his Lordship insulted him, and called him a liar, and swore he would not believe anybody but the surgeon, Kirkland. Upon being again assured that he was dead, he desired that the people might be dispersed, saying that he would surrender; yet, almost in the same breath, he desired that the people might be let in, and have some victuals and drink; but the issue was that he went away again from the window, swearing that he would not be taken. The people, however, still continued near the house, and two hours later he was seen on the bowling-green by one Cortis, a collier. 'My Lord' was then armed with a blunderbus and a dagger, and two or three pistols; but Curtis, so far from being intimidated .... marched boldly up to him, and his Lordship was so struck with the determinate resolution shown by this brave fellow, that he suffered him to seize him without making any resistance. Yet the moment that he was in custody he declared that he had killed a villain, and that he gloried in the deed."

The rest of the story is soon told. From Staunton Lord Ferrers was taken to Ashby, where he was kept at an inn till the Monday following. During the interval, a coroner's jury sat upon the body, bringing in a verdict of "wilful murder." From Ashby Lord Ferrers was sent to gaol at Leicester, and thence, about a fortnight later, to London. He was brought up, we are told, in his own landau and six, under a strong guard. He arrived in town about noon on the 14th of February, "dressed like a jockey, in a close riding frock, jockey boots and cap, and a plain shirt."

Being arraigned before the House of Lords—for a peer has a legal right to be tried by his peers—and the coroner's verdict having been read aloud, he was formally committed into the custody of the Usher of the Black Rod, and ordered to be kept in the Tower. He arrived there about six in the evening, and we are gravely told that " he behaved during the whole journey and at his commitment with great exactness and propriety"—whatever those words may mean. It may interest Mr. Hepworth Dixon, as the author of "Her Majesty's Tower," to learn on good authority that he was confined in the Round Tower near the drawbridge, two warders being constantly in the room with him, and one at the door; "two sentinels also were posted on the stairs, and one upon the drawbridge, with their bayonets fixed; and from this time the gates were ordered to be shut an hour sooner than usual." It is strange that so much of extra precaution should have been taken because a culprit about to be tried for his life happened to have worn an earl's coronet.

We are told by the chronicler of small things relating to this titled prisoner of State, how much beer, how much porter, how much water Lord Ferrers was allowed daily during his incarceration. No doubt the writer "interviewed"—

or at least tried to interview—the noble Earl in his dungeon. Mrs. C——, his lady-housekeeper, and her four young children were allowed to see him from time to time, and to correspond with him daily from a lodging which they had taken in the neighbourhood of the Minories.

On the 16th of April, when he had been a prisoner a little more than two months, he was brought to trial at the bar of the House of Peers. Lord Henley, afterwards Earl of Northington, who at that time happened to be Keeper of the Great Seal, presided as Lord High Steward, but with a want of dignity to which Horace Walpole more than once alludes in his letters to Sir Horace Mann and Mr. George Montague. The trial lasted till the 18th, when Lord Ferrers endeavoured with great skill and cleverness to elicit from several witnesses proofs of his insanity. No detailed report of the substance of such examination is extant; but it may easily be believed that the greater the skill that he displayed the more signal his failure.

"His Lordship," says one account, "managed his defence in such a manner as to show perfect recollection of mind and uncommon powers of understanding; he dwelt with the most delicate and affecting sensibility on the hard situation of being reduced to the necessity of proving himself a lunatic in order that he might not be deemed a murderer; and when at last he found that his plea could avail him nothing, he confessed that he had put it forward only to gratify his friends, being always averse to it himself."

It is needless to add that each of his brother peers, on being asked the usual question, brought in against Lord Ferrers a verdict of " Guilty upon my honour;" accordingly he was sentenced by Lord Henley, in due form, to be hanged by the neck till he was dead," and that his body should be given afterwards, as was then the usual practice, to the anatomists for dissection. The day at first fixed for the execution was the 21st of April; but we are told that, " in consideration of his rank," the fatal hour was postponed to the 5th of May. It seems more to the point to record the fact that, also " in consideration of his rank," he was permitted to be hanged with a silken instead of a hempen rope.

At the trial, not only the Earl himself, but his two brothers, tried to prove him to have inherited the family misfortune of insanity; and, as Horace Walpole remarks, " it must have been a strange contradiction to see a man trying, by his own sense, to prove himself out of his senses, and even more shocking to see his two brothers brought to prove the lunacy of their own blood, in order to save their brother's life. Both," adds the old gossiper, "are almost as ill-looking men as the Earl; one of them is a clergyman suspended by the Bishop of London for being a methodist; the other a wild vagabond, whom they call in the country 'ragged and dangerous.'" As a proof of the madness of Lord Ferrers himself, it may be mentioned that two years before, in 1758, he attempted to murder his wife, "a pretty, harmless young woman," according to Horace Walpole.

During the interval between his sentence and its execution, his lordship made a will bequeathing various sums to Mrs. C——, to his children by her, and to the children of his victim—a poor instalment of the reparation which he owed to the orphans for the murder of their parent.

The scaffold was erected at Tyburn turnpike, as nearly as possible on the spot where now stand Connaught-place and Connaught-square. About nine o'clock on the morning of the 5th his lordship's person was formally demanded of the keeper of the Tower by the sheriffs of London and Middlesex. Being informed of the fact, Lord Ferrers requested that he might be allowed to travel to Tyburn in his own landau, instead of in the mourning coach which had been provided. His request was granted; and at the gate of the Tower he entered for the last time his own "landau," accompanied by one of the sheriffs and by the chaplain of the Tower, one Mr. Humphries.

The account of the journey from the Tower to Tyburn, as it stands in the *Gentleman's Magazine*, is so strange that I venture to extract it entire:

"He was dressed in a suit of light-coloured clothes, embroidered with silver, said to have been his wedding suit; and soon after the sheriff entered the landau he said, "You may perhaps, sir, think it strange to see me in this dress, but I have my particular reasons for it." The procession then began in the following order: A very large body of constables of the county of Middlesex, preceded by one of the high constables: a party of horse grenadiers and a party of foot; Mr. Sheriff Errington in his chariot, accompanied by his under-sheriff, Mr. Jackson; the landau, escorted by two other parties of horse grenadiers and foot; Mr. Sheriff Vaillant's chariot, in which was the under-sheriff Mr. Nichols; a mourning coach and six, with some of his Lordship's friends; and lastly a hearse and six, provided for the conveyance of his Lordship's corpse from the place of execution to Surgeons' Hall."

It is added that—

"The procession moved so slow that Lord Ferrers was two hours and three-quarters in his landau; but during the whole time he appeared perfectly easy and composed, though he often expressed his desire to have it over, saying that the apparatus of death and the passing through such crowds of people was ten times worse than death itself. He told the sheriff that he had written to the King, begging that he might suffer where his ancestor, the Earl of Essex, had suffered—namely, on Tower Hill; that 'he had been in the greater hope of obtaining this favour as he had the honour of quartering part of the same arms and of being allied to his Majesty; and that he thought it hard that he should have to die at the place appointed for the execution of common felons.' As to his crime, he declared that he did it 'under particular circumstances, having met with so many crosses and vexations that he scarcely knew what he did;' and in fine he protested that he had not the least malice towards Mr. Johnson."

It would be profitless to dwell on all the lesser details of Lord Ferrers' last journey—how he felt thirsty as he passed the top of Drury-lane, and wanted a glass of wine and water before he went on; how he gave a sovereign to the assistant-executioner in mistake for his principal; how he declared to the chaplain that he believed in a God, but did not like "sectaries" and their teaching; how he expressed at the last moment his forgiveness of the hangman and of all mankind.

It is enough to say, in the words of "Sylvanus Urban," whose contributor was doubtless an eye-witness of the scene, that his Lordship met his fate with fortitude and composure of mind as he was pinioned and had the cap drawn over his eyes, and that as soon as the bolt was withdrawn the drop fell, and Lord Ferrers died quickly and with but little apparent pain. At the end of an hour the body was put into a coffin, and taken to Surgeons' Hall, where the remainder of the sentence was carried out in all its disgusting details. The corpse, thus mutilated, was publicly exposed to view, and on the Thursday following was handed to his Lordship's friends and family for interment; but his remains were not destined to rest with those of his ancesters at Staunton Harold, for Mr. John Timbs tells us in his 'Curiosities of London' that after his execution, the body of Lord Ferrers was taken to old St. Pancras church and there buried privately beneath the belfry, in a grave fourteen feet deep.

The Earl's widow also met with a tragic fate. She married, secondly, Lord F. Campbell, brother of John, fifth Duke of Argyll, and was burnt to death at Coombe Bank, Kent, in 1807, aged seventy years.

Horace Walpole calls Lord Ferrers "a low wretch, a mad assassin, and a wild beast;" and he details all the circumstances of his trial and execution with considerable minuteness to Sir Horace Mann, then our ambassador at Florence. "What," he asks, "will your Italians say to a peer of England, an earl of one of our best families, tried for murdering his servant with the utmost solemnity, and then hanged at the common place for the execution of highwaymen, and afterwards anatomised?"

I will only add that as Lord Ferrers had no legitimate issue, the title and estate passed to his brother, and that therefore the present Earl Ferrers and the various collateral branches of the house of Shirley can at all events boast that they do not inherit one drop of the blood of Laurence, third Earl Ferrers.

THE DUCHESS OF KINGSTON.

AMONG the ladies of "Quality" who made themselves most conspicuous and famous—I may almost say *famosæ* in the classical sense of the term—in the good old days when George III. was King, was Elizabeth Chudleigh, Countess of Bristol, and (or) Duchess of Kingston. A proud, haughty, and imperious child, she grew up headstrong and self-willed beyond her fellows, in an age when independence of character was far from uncommon among women; and it is clear that she reigned for many years, feared, if not loved, among the circle of her compeers, long before her name was brought prominently before the world by certain events which I purpose recording in the present paper.

In the early part of the last century a certain Colonel and Mrs. Chudleigh were living at the Royal Hospital, Chelsea, where the former, a cadet of a good family in Devonshire, and who had served in the army under Marlborough, held a subordinate post. Mr. and Mrs. Chudleigh had a family of several sons and daughters, the eldest of whom Elizabeth, was, as Horace Walpole tells us, one of his playmates when he lived in his father's house at Chelsea.*

Colonel Chudleigh died early, leaving it to his relict to educate and "bring out" into society his young family on a very small income, exclusive of her pension as an officer's widow. Under these circumstances Mrs. Chudleigh appears to have done what most other women would do in

---

* Horace Walpole set her down as being fifty-five or fifty-six at the time of her trial, and he was likely to know the fact, as she and her brothers were his playfellows. The Walpoles then lived at Chelsea, and her father, Colonel Thomas Chudleigh (who died in 1726) was Deputy Governor of the College. Her mother was something of a heroine in her way; at all events, the story is told that, being asleep one night as she was returning from a late party between London and Chelsea, she was awakened suddenly by three footpads, one of whom held a pistol to her breast. She coolly put her head out of the other window of her carriage, and said "Fire," when the patrol, who were fortunately at hand, fired, and shot the robber. The daughter, if we may judge from the coolness and nerve which she displayed on the memorable trial in Westminster Hall, was quite a "chip of the old block," and in no way degenerate.

a like position, and resolved to turn to account her own and her husband's " good connections" —the best substitute for money. She hired a house on the outskirts of the town, within reach of the rival camps of St. James's and Kensington Palaces; and, if she did not seek, at all events she soon found, an opportunity of displaying in high quarters the charms and attractions of her eldest daughter Elizabeth, who was almost a woman at fifteen. From a child, it is said, she was distinguished for a brilliancy of wit and repartee,* and for other qualities which shone more brightly in fashionable circles than at home. It so happened that Frederick Prince of Wales and the Princess (the father and mother of George III.) held their Court at Leicester House, on the north side of what now is Leicester Square, having quitted St. James's in consequence of the continual quarrels between the Prince and his parents. Mr. Pulteney, afterwards Earl of Bath, was at this time a great favourite of the Prince and Princess. The Chudleighs knew something

* As an example of her wit, we may mention the following anecdote, which is told by Sir N. W. Wraxall. The Princess of Wales—who was accused of being far too intimate with Lord Bute—one day took Miss Chudleigh to task for some act of levity. "*Ah, Madame,*" was her quick retort, "*chacune ici a son But.*"

of Mr. Pulteney or of his wife, and Elizabeth, through their interest, was appointed when only just eighteen one of the Maids of Honour to the Princess. Mr. Pulteney took a somewhat more than paternal interest in the clever girl, and encouraged her to improve her education, which had been somewhat neglected, and made her his amanuensis and constant correspondent. To him she would read aloud, and, although her volatile disposition prevented her from ever seriously applying herself to study, she gained sufficient superficial information to enable her to fulfil her own avowed aim of being on all subjects, whether she wrote or spoke, " short, clear, and surprising."

Had she lived in our days she would probably have become a lady novelist; as it was, she played a *rôle* of her own choosing, acting out a romance instead of writing one. With such a pupil even so grave a statesman as Pulteney could laugh and amuse himself, for she had always plenty of small talk at hand; but it must be owned that when he tried to initiate her into the secrets of political economy and statesmanship, she rather demurred, and showed a decided preference for literature of a more amusing kind, and probably for lighter and more frivolous diversions. In her station, with a pretty face, fine figure, and much ready wit to recommend her, Miss Chudleigh soon became a general favourite with the Court at "Leicester Fields," among whom she could laugh and sing and play a part in the miniature theatre as well as any of the rest. A host of admirers sprung up around her, some with coronets in possession, others with titles in prospect.

Among those who were struck with her beauty and fascination was the Duke of Hamilton, who subsequently wedded one of the beautiful Miss Gunnings, after whom all the world ran mad, as already stated. The Duke proposed and was accepted, and it seemed as if she were about to attain the summit of her ambition, the ducal strawberry leaves, when the machinations of a heartless and meddlesome relative, Mrs. Hanmer, dashed the cup of happiness from her lips. Whatever may have been the motive of Mrs. Hanmer's dislike to the Hamiltons, it is certain that she set herself deliberately to work to break off the engagement of her niece, and to destroy her prospects by intercepting the letters of the Duke during his temporary absence in France. Like many another young lady's heart, that of Miss Chudleigh, if she had one, was caught on the rebound. It is probable that her ambition received a more severe blow than her affections in the supposed neglect of the Duke. Like the Duc de Roussillon's pet widow, "she would be a Duchess;" and a Duchess in some sort, at least in England, though not in Scotland, she was destined to become, although the intrigues of her aunt prevented her from sharing the honours of his Grace of Hamilton.

Among the daily visitors of her aunt was a young naval officer, the Honourable Augustus Hervey, of whom Mrs. Hanmer was very fond, and on whom she had, for some inscrutable reason, fixed to become the husband of her niece. It was easy to throw the pretty, heedless girl into the young sailor's way, and to persuade the insulted beauty that the Duke's neglect proved he had ceased to care for her, at the same time contrasting his conduct with the devotion of her new admirer, and artfully suggesting that Hervey was in ultimate remainder to the Earldom of Bristol. The bait took; her hopes of becoming a Duchess being for the time frustrated, Elizabeth Chudleigh elected to run the chance of wearing a Countess's coronet, although she cared nothing for the man who was to confer it on her.

Urged on the one side by the dictates of wounded pride and disappointed ambition, and on the other by the worldly arguments of an artful woman, Miss Chudleigh consented in an evil hour to become the wife of Captain Hervey; but as neither she nor her lover could afford the loss of her place at Court, it was settled that the marriage should be strictly private, and that even afterwards she should still officiate in her capacity as a "maid of honour."

In the neighbourhood of Winchester there is a small parish named Lainston, and here in a private chapel adjoining the house of the squire, Mr. Merrill, was celebrated the union between Captain Hervey and Miss Chudleigh. It was celebrated late in the evening, by the light of a tallow candle stuck into an empty bottle, and without much ceremony. The consequences of such a marriage, with no fixed principles of right and wrong on the part of either, could not be otherwise than most disastrous. Captain Hervey seems, indeed, to have been utterly devoid of any qualities which could ensure the esteem of or attach even temporarily such a woman as Elizabeth Chudleigh; and her miseries, which date from this ill-starred union, proved the cause of all the future unhappiness which dogged her steps through life and gave a colour to her fate. Only some forty-eight hours had elapsed from the scene in the little chapel when the bride and bridegroom parted; and, as the union had not been publicly notified, they agreed that it should be kept secret. Elizabeth had already had sufficient knowledge of her husband's disposition to be aware it would require all the art of which she was mistress to insure his discretion should he change his mind and propose to make the marriage public. The best argument which she could plead was the fact that he had little or nothing to live on but his pay, and that if her marriage was publicly known she would lose her post as maid of honour. He therefore yielded the point, but in a way which showed that he was resolved to play the tyrant and to torture his victim. In fact, as she often expressed herself, "Her misery began with the arrival of Mr. Hervey in England, and the greatest joy that she experienced was the news of his departure." Hence, while his ship was in the Downs or at Spithead, she always trembled with fear lest his destination might be altered by orders from the Lords of the Admiralty. "A fair wind down the Channel" was the soother of her mind, and nothing pleased her better than to hear that his ship had been "spoken" leagues away from England on the wide Atlantic.

Miss Chudleigh, or rather Mrs. Hervey, for such she was in the eye of the law—a maid in appearance, but really a wife in disguise,—came back to London, and mixed as usual in the highest circles, with a cheerful face, but a heart heavy with the consciousness of her anomalous position and a prescience of the misfortunes which awaited her. Her husband, though quieted for a time, made his presence in London offensively known, and even contrived to visit her at her lodgings in Maddox Street. Not many months afterwards Miss Chudleigh gave birth to a son, who, however, lived only a few short weeks. The same thing happened again a year or two later, and for some little time there was a boy who, if he had grown to manhood, would have "put out of joint" the nose of the subsequent Earls and Marquises of Bristol. About this time, to add to the chagrins of the unhappy young wife, the Duke of Hamilton returned from France, and hastened to throw himself at the feet of his lady love, and to inquire the reason of her mysterious silence. Mutual explanations ensued, and it appeared that, so far from his affection for Miss Chudleigh having cooled, he was more than ever desirous of making her his wife without delay. To his surprise his suit was peremptorily rejected, and it being in fact equally impossible for the *ci-devant* Miss Chudleigh either to accept him, or to explain her reasons for refusing the object of her former ambition, she was subjected to much inconvenient importunity from her mother, as well as from the Duke.

To escape the reproaches and resentment of the former, who, all this time was wholly ignorant of the fact of her daughter's marriage with Mr. Hervey, and of her having become a mother, she next embarked for the Continent, where, says Hone in his "Year Book," she lived in a style of shameless dissipation. Calling herself Miss Chudleigh, she now so wrought upon Frederick the Great that he dispensed with all etiquette, in consequence of her request that "she might study at her ease a prince who gave lessons to all Europe, and who might boast of having an admirer in every individual of the British nation." During her residence at Berlin she was treated with the greatest distinction. She afterwards went to Dresden, where she obtained the friendship of the Electress, who loaded her with presents. Upon returning to England, she resumed her attendance upon the Princess of Wales, and continued to be the attraction of the Court. Her marriage with Captain Hervey, however, perpetually annoyed her, and, to destroy all trace of it, she went with a party of friends to the parish where it had been celebrated, and, having asked for the register book, tore out the record of her marriage while the clergyman was in conversation with the rest of the party.

Shortly afterwards, Captain Hervey becoming Earl of Bristol by the death of his father, and a rumour prevailing that he was in a declining state of health, Miss Chudleigh, now Countess of Bristol, hoping to be soon a wealthy dowager, obtained the restoration of the entry in the register. Fortune, however, was against her, and she found that by her precipitate act she had outwitted herself; as, to her great disappointment, the Earl her husband took it into his head to recover his health and strength, and she found herself once more a wife, and yet not a wife.

How far her marriage with Mr. Hervey had ever leaked out into the ears of "society" is not very clear; but it is an axiom in the highest circles, I believe, that, as sin is not sin in the "elect" of Calvin, so "*vice is not vice in a duchess.*" And, therefore, even if the real state of the case was known to some of her friends, there was no one at hand to "forbid the banns," when, in March, 1769, she publicly married Evelyn Pierrepont, Duke of Kingston, a not very wise old gentleman, who was somewhat of an invalid, and whose death might be expected in the course of nature at no distant date.

While the arrangements for this second alliance were pending, she made a variety of unavailing proposals to Lord Bristol to agree to a divorce, and even offered to facilitate it by some flagrant misconduct of her own before the eyes of all. But he refused. Luckily, however, the Earl found another lady who pleased him better, having plenty of cash at her banker's; and in the course of a few months a sentence of divorce was pronounced by the Ecclesiastical Courts at Doctors'-Commons, and the marriage was solemnised as I have related.

Elizabeth Chudleigh was now at all events, if not a countess, at least an honest woman, and (which she valued still more highly) a duchess. She had gained the height of her ambition, and a giddy height she found it. She had but mounted

"Unde altior esset
Casus et impulsæ præceps immane ruinæ."

The Duke very kindly and conveniently lived long enough to establish her fairly in the eyes of the world as his Duchess, and then—"died and slept with his fathers." On opening his Grace's will it was found that he had bequeathed to her his entire property, upon condition that she should never marry again; and the Duchess plunged into a course of licentiousness which exposed her to public censure, and in consequence of which she went to Italy. A magnificent yacht, built and ornamented at an immense expense, conveyed her to Rome, where she was received with great pomp by the Pope and Cardinals, who knew but little of her antecedents, and treated as a princess. During her residence in Rome she was on the eve of bestowing her hand and fortune upon an adventurer, who represented himself to be the Prince of Albania, when he was apprehended as a swindler, and committed suicide in prison. Soon afterwards, she learned that the heirs of the Duke of Kingston sought to establish against her the charge of bigamy, in order to invalidate her marriage with the Duke, and set aside his will. She instantly repaired to her banker, who, having been gained over by the other party, concealed himself, to avoid giving her the sum requisite for a journey to London. She placed herself at his door, and, pistol in hand, compelled him to comply with her demand. Upon her arrival in England she found that her first marriage had been declared valid, upon the ground of incompetency in the court which had pronounced it void. Public opinion was against her; and, under the character of Lady Kitty Crocodile, she was ridiculed by Foote in a comedy entitled "A Trip to Calais," of which, however, she succeeded in obtaining the prohibition from the Lord Chamberlain.

The validity of her first marriage with Mr. Hervey at Lainston having been established by witnesses who were present, to the satisfaction of those of the Duke's relatives who had an interest in setting aside his will, it was resolved that she should be publicly indicted for bigamy, and that her trial should be really a state trial, being held in Westminster Hall, the House of Peers sitting as her judges.

Finding it necessary to return to England, as already stated, in order to meet the charges which were being made publicly against her, the Duchess embarked for Dover, and reaching London, drove straight to her house at Knightsbridge, where she found plenty of friends ready to espouse her cause—amongst others the Earl of Mansfield and the Duke of Newcastle. Anxious, apparently, to turn to the best account the weary weeks which must intervene before the day of the trial, and to advertise herself, and to rouse if possible the men in her cause, even if she scandalised the fairer portion of creation, she resolved to put in her appearance once more in some place of public resort, and accordingly the next night she attended a masked ball at the residence of Mrs. Cornelys, at Carlisle House, Soho-square.

She appeared on this occasion as 'Iphigenia'. There is a print which represents her in this character, and which fully justifies the sarcastic terms in which Horace Walpole alludes to it.

Meanwhile the attention of the world was concentrated on the expected trial, to which Horace Walpole often alludes in a vein of banter which shows that he considered the Duchess no better than she ought to be. He writes to his friend Sir Horace Mann, in Italy, March 22, in that year: "Everybody is on the quest for tickets for her Grace of Kingston's trial. I am persuaded that her impudence will operate in some singular manner; probably she will appear in weeds, with a train to reach across Westminster Hall, with mourning maids of honour to support her when she swoons at her dear Duke's name, and in a black veil to conceal her blushing— or not blushing. To this farce, novel and curious as it will be, I shall not go. I think cripples have no business in crowds, but at the Pool of Bethesda; and to be sure this is no angel that troubles the waters."

The trial was a matter which, for weeks before it came on, absorbed the public attention to an extent which has never since been equalled, except by the trial of the impostor Orton who wanted to palm himself off as a Tichborne. It was attended by Queen Charlotte, the Prince of Wales, by most of the members of the Royal

Family, the foreign ambassadors, Members of Parliament, and other distinguished personages. The Duchess, in deep mourning, took her seat unmoved, attended by two *femmes de chambre*, a physician, an apothecary, her secretary, and a formidable army of defenders in the shape of six barristers in wig and gown. I have before me a picture of the Duchess standing at the bar and pleading her own cause; and if, as I have reason to think, it is a sketch from life, there can be no doubt that she was a woman well able to hold her own, even before the most august assembly in England.

As usual, it is from the chatty pages of Horace Walpole that we learn nearly all that is known of the way in which "society" at the time regarded the trial of her Grace the Duchess of Kingston. He did not go actually to see it or hear it, for he "hated crowds," and viewed the chief actor or actress with no favourable eye; but he describes the scene in Westminster Hall almost as vividly as if he had been present in this letter to Sir Horace Mann, April 17, 1776:

"We think and talk but of one subject—the solemn comedy that is acting in Westminster Hall. Deep wagers had been laid that the Duchess would decamp before the trial came on. This, with a million of other stories, has been so spread that I am determined to believe no one fact but what I shall read in the printed trial; for at it I have not been, though curious enough about so august a mummery and so original a culprit. . . . The scene opened on Wednesday with all its pomp . . . and the doubly noble prisoner went through her part with universal admiration. Instead of her usual ostentatious folly and clumsy pretensions to cunning, all her conduct was decent, and even seemed natural. Her dress was entirely black and plain; her attendants not too numerous; her dismay at first perfectly unaffected. A few tears balanced cheerfulness enough, and her presence of mind and attention never deserted her. This rational behaviour and the pleadings of her four counsel, who contended for the finality of her Ecclesiastical Court's sentence against a second trial, carried her triumphantly through the first day, and turned the stream much in her favour."

The next day she was less successful, and, in consequence, " had to be blooded as soon as she retired, and fell into a great passion of tears." And probably Horace Walpole, at this time, was not singular in thinking that the Ecclesiastical Courts were quite as much on their trial as was her Grace. He adds that Lord Bristol, in his opinion, did not stand in a fair predicament, for he had never avowed his marriage with Miss Chudleigh, and was supposed to have connived for a sum of money at her marrying the Duke.

Ever alive to the last floating rumours and the gossip of the day, Horace writes to the Rev. W. Mason, under date April 20, 1776: "The plot thickens, or rather opens. Yesterday the judges were called on for their opinions, and *unâ voce* dismantled the Ecclesiastical Court." . . . The Attorney-General, Thurlow, then detailed the "Life and Adventures of Elizabeth Chudleigh, *alias* Hervey, *alias* the most high and puissante princess the Duchess of Kingston." Her Grace bore the narration with a front worthy of her exalted rank. Then was produced the first capital witness, the ancient damsel who was present at her first marriage. . . . To this witness her Grace was benign, but had a transitory swoon at the mention of her dear Duke's name; and at intervals has been blooded enough to have supplied her execution, if necessary. Two babes were likewise proved to have blessed her first nuptials, one of whom, for aught that appears, may exist and become Earl of Bristol."

The register of Chelsea old church has certainly the following entry, Nov. 2, 1747: "Augustus Hervey, son of the Hon. Augustus Hervey, baptised by the Hon. and Rev. Henry Aston;" and the discovery of this entry, as Lysons observes, might have spared many interrogatories at the Duchess of Kingston's trial.

The trial lasted through several days; on Friday the 19th and Saturday the 20th the case of the Duchess did not gain ground at all, but rather the reverse. So much so indeed was this the case, that one of her friends remarked that she must have been mad "to have sought the trial, or not to have poisoned the witnesses." For instance, there appeared a maid who was present at her first marriage. Serjeant Hawkins authenticated the birth of at least one child; and the widow of the parson who officiated at her first marriage, and on whom she forced a fictitious register when she expected Lord Bristol's death and had a mind to be a countess, deposed that, though privy to all these circumstances, on visiting her as Duchess the latter said to her, "Well, Mrs. Phillips, was not the Duke very good to marry an old maid like me?"

And what, the reader will ask, was the end of this memorable trial? Elizabeth Chudleigh was found guilty by the House of Peers, but, " pleading her privilege" as a peer's wife, she was discharged without any punishment.

On the 23rd of April Walpole writes to his

friend Mason: "The wisdom of the land has been exerted for five days in turning a duchess into a countess, and yet does not think it a punishable crime for a countess to convert herself into a duchess. After a paltry defence, and a speech of fifty pages (which she had herself written, and pronounced very well), the sages, in spite of the Attorney-General (who brandished a hot iron), dismissed her with the single injunction of paying the fees, all voting her guilty, but the Duke of Newcastle—her neighbour in the country—softening his vote by adding 'erroneously, not intentionally.' So ends the solemn farce. "The Earl of Bristol, they say," adds Walpole, "does not intend to leave her that title, nor the house of Medows a shilling. . . . I am glad to have done with her."

Hannah More, who was present among the crowd, tells us that she was dressed in deep mourning, but that hardly a trace of her once enchanting beauty was visible, and that if it had not been for her white face, she might easily have been taken for a bale of bombasin. She adds that she behaved herself properly and even with dignity, and that her presence of mind did not desert her for a single moment.

Undeterred by the threat of a writ *ne exeat regno* being issued against her, as soon as the trial was over the Duchess-countess was off to Calais, and on her way to Paris. She writes from Calais on the 26th to a friend, sarcastically remarking that the peers have recognised her as Countess of Bristol, the Ecclesiastical Courts as duchess, but that she still adhered to her own position, and proudly signed her name to the letter "Elizabeth, Duchesse de Kingston." She retired to Paris "incontinently," as the phrase then ran; and the writ *ne exeat regno* was issued just after the bird was flown. Probably her enemies took good care not to drive her too closely into a corner, and felt that it was better for the peace of London, and of "society," that she should be on the other side of the Channel. "Don't let us talk of her any more," writes Horace Walpole; he adds in the same breath, "Yes, I must say a word more. I will tell you what the droll Lord Abercorn said. Somebody 'hoped that his Lordship had not suffered by the trial.' He replied, 'Oh no, nobody suffered by it.' And, indeed, though not a comedy, it was a farce."

The subsequent career of the ex-Duchess was in keeping with her preceding adventures. I have already mentioned that she was too sharp for the writ *ne exeat regno,* and before it could be issued she had bolted from Knightsbridge, and turned up at Calais, though there were no railways or steamers to aid her flight. From Calais she made her way to Rome, where she contrived to propitiate the favour of the Pope so far as to be received by him and fêted *en princesse*—a good turn which she requited by a handsome bequest of jewelry in her will.

After remaining there for some time she returned to Calais, and hired a spacious mansion, which she furnished splendidly; but, the monotony of the town not suiting her volatile and turbulent disposition, she made a voyage to St Petersburg in a magnificent yacht, and was received with the highest distinction by the Empress Catherine, to whom she presented the valuable collection of pictures formed by the Kingston family. She afterwards went to Poland, where Prince Radzivil gave sumptuous entertainments in honour of her visit, particularly a bear hunt by torchlight. Upon returning to France she purchased the beautiful château de Sainte Assize, two leagues from Fontainebleau, and a mansion at the Rue Coq Héron at Paris, where she died in 1788, after executing a will, made by two attorneys who came from England on purpose. She bequeathed a set of jewels to the Empress of Russia, a large diamond to the Pope, and a costly pearl necklace and earrings to the Countess of Salisbury, because they had belonged to a lady who bore that title in the reign of Henry IV. Her property in France was estimated at £200,000 sterling, besides which she had valuable possessions in England and Russia.

The Duchess of Kingston, during her second *noces* and in her second widowhood, lived at Kingston House, Knightsbridge, afterwards known as Listowel House, and at one time the residence of the Marquis Wellesley. In allusion to her connection with this spot, she is spoken of in a play of the last century as "the notified Bet Cheatley, Duchess of Knightsbridge." Peter Cunningham, in his "Handbook of London," briefly and tersely disposes of her as "the profligate and eccentric Duchess." Leigh Hunt, in his "Old Court Suburb," styles her "an adventuress, who after playing tricks with a parish register for the purpose of alternately falsifying and substantiating a real marriage, according as the prospects of her husband varied, imposed herself upon a duke for a spinster, and survived him as a duchess until unmasked in a court of law." He adds his opinion that she was "a well-born and handsome, but coarse-minded woman, qualified to impose on none but very young or very shallow admirers. Her first husband, who became Earl of Bristol, was at the time of his marriage with her a young seaman just out of his teens; and the Duke, her second husband, though he was the nephew of Lady Mary Wortley Montague, appears never to have outgrown the teens of his understanding." Mr. Leigh Hunt thus wittily and pithily expresses his opinion about her: "Hating prolixity and mock modesty, her maxim . . . was to be 'short, clear, and surprising;' so she concentrated her rhetoric into swearing, and dressed in a style next door to nakedness. The wealth, however, which was bequeathed to her by the Duke enabled her, in spite of the loss of his title in England, to go and flare as a duchess abroad, where her jewels procured for her the friendship of sovereigns, and the Pope himself figured in her will."

For my own part, I venture to think that she may have had, and probably had *au fond* a good and noble disposition, accompanied, however, with a high and proud spirit and strong passions. The cruel deceit practised on her when young by her aunt, coupled with her intense ambition, her waywardness, and her pride, perverted the better part of her nature, and drove her into courses from which in the innocence of childhood and youth she would have shrunk back with horror.

There is a sense of awful responsibility in the

reflection that we all exercise an influence, more or less, for good or evil on those around us; and for those who misuse it to warp the ductile minds of the young in order to carry out their own selfish purposes a fearful day of reckoning will surely come, when they will plead in vain, "Am I my brother's keeper?" Such at least is the moral that I would have my readers draw from the story of Elizabeth Chudleigh.

Mr Addison, in his "Anecdotes," tells an amusing story of the Duchess, showing that she was proud and haughty, and had far too high a sense of her dignity. Being one day detained in her carriage by a cart of coals that was unloading in a very narrow street, she leaned out with both her arms upon the door, and asked the fellow, "How dare you, sirrah, to stop a woman of quality in the street?" "Woman of quality!" replied the man. "Yes, fellow," rejoined her Grace ;" don't you see *my arms upon my carriage?*" "Yes, I do indeed," he answered, "and a pair of d—d coarse arms they are."

THE DRUMMONDS, EARLS OF PERTH.

FEW names, even in Scottish history, stand forward more nobly and well-known than that of Drummond. According to Sir Bernard Burke and the heralds, the house of Drummond derives its descent from a Hungarian in the suite of Edgar Atheling, the cotemporary, and in some sense rival, of William the Conqueror; but the importance of the family dates really from the reign of Robert III. of Scotland, who took for his consort Lady Annabella, a fair daughter of Drummond of Stobhall. From that period they became closely connected with the Court and the Crown of Scotland, and attained the honours of the peerage of that country nearly four hundred years ago, in A.D. 1487, when the head of the house, Sir John Drummond, of Cargill and Stobhall, a distinguished statesman and diplomatist of his day, and Ambassador Exrtaordinary to the Court of St. James, was created Lord Drummond: his great-great-grandson, James fourth Lord, being Ambassador for King James VI. to Spain, was created in 1605, Earl of Perth, with remainder to his " heirs male whomsoever."

The story of the origin of the name of Drummond is thus related in the older Peerages: " Maurice, son of George, son of Andrew, King of Hungary, being in command of the vessel in which Saint Margaret, afterwards Queen of Malcolm III., embarked for Hungary, happened to be driven by a storm into the Frith of Forth. Here, on landing, fortune befriended him, for he was made Steward of Lennox, and received from the hands of King Malcolm the lands of Drymen, or Drummen, from which was derived the name of Drummond. And to this day, in memory of his safe pilotage of Queen Margaret, his descendants bear for their arms ' three bars wavy, gules,' representing the waves of the sea."

His descendant in the fifth generation, Sir John Drummond of Drummond, and Steward or Thane of Lennox, was a brave defender of the liberties of Scotland at the commencement of King Edward's usurpation; and his son, Sir Malcolm, immediately after the Battle of Bannockburn, obtained from Robert I. a grant of broad lands in Perthshire, in reward of his services in that battle, in which by his advice caltrops were first used as a defence against the English horse. In memory of this sage counsel "his descendants," as Burke tells us, "bear caltrops upon a compartment with their arms, along with the motto, 'Gang warily.'"

His grandson, Sir John Drummond, marrying a lady named De Pontifex, heiress of Stobhall and other extensive estates in Perthshire, became by her the father of a daughter, the Lady Annabella, a lady of great beauty and merit, whom we have already mentioned as the wife of King Robert III. She was crowned with him, as Queen Consort of Scotland, in September, 1390; and it is worthy of note that her blood runs in the veins not merely of Queen Victoria, but of many other crowned heads of Europe in this our nineteenth century.

It is not my purpose here to give an exact account of all the achievements of all the Lords of Drummond and Earls of Perth. It is enough to say that, in the words of one of the members of that House, Lady Clementina Davies, in her "Recollections of Society," they "first suffered exile and losses in common with the Stuarts, whom they regarded as their only true Sovereigns; and then, after a hundred years of exile at St. Germain, they shared the fall and misfortunes of the House of Bourbon, to which they had been scarcely less loyally attached."

This claim, advanced by Lady C. Davies, is supported by the independent testimony of Burke, who observes: " Their loyalty (*i. e.* that of the Drummonds) to the throne shone at all times conspicuous, but the crisis which called out their whole energies and devotion was the great contest which preceded the final overthrow of the ancient dynasty of Scotland, that of the Stuarts. So long as the conflict was waged on the battle field the Drummonds fought manfully in the cause which they had espoused, and, at length, when the last ruin of the hapless cause of Stuart was consummated at Culloden, they left their native land, to die banished and broken-hearted in a foreign clime. They had fearlessly set their all upon the cast of the die, and they cheerfully submitted to its hazard."

And such really was the case; James, the fourth Earl of Perth, on the defeat and abdication of King James II., accompanied his Sovereign into exile at St. Germain. He was Lord Chancellor of Scotland, and a man of high standing in the world of politics as well as of law; he was also connected with the noblest of the Scottish houses, his three wives having been respectively the daughter of the Marquis of Douglas, the widow of the Earl of Tullibardine, and the daughter of the Marquis of Huntly, head of the Ducal House of Gordon. His fidelity to the Stuarts was not unrewarded, as he was raised by James in 1695, to the Dukedom of Perth, a title which was confirmed in France by Louis XIV. on the death of James, along with the other Dukedoms of Berwick, Fitzjames, Albemarle and Melfort. He died just before the Scottish rising of 1715.

But I must pass on to another part of the story of the Drummonds, that of the second Duke of Perth and of his gallant Duchess. History tells us how James, fifth Earl and second Duke of Perth, fought by the side of King James at the Battle of the Boyne, at Limerick, and at Londonderry, and remaining with him till all his hopes were defeated, returned to Scotland in 1692. While his father lay a prisoner in Stirling Castle, he crossed over to France, and was made Master of the Horse to Mary of Modena, James's Queen. Next, returning to Scotland, we find him opposing the Union with all his might; and, in 1715, he joined the standard of rebellion raised by the Earl of Mar and his Highland chieftains, and commanded the cavalry at the Battle of Sheriffmuir. His wife was Lady

Jean Gordon, a daughter of the Duke of Gordon, whose story I here relate.

"Both by family descent—her father and her mother being strict Roman Catholics—and also in virtue of her marriage, her Grace had imbibed a spirit of entire devotion to the Stuart cause. She is described, in a contemporary pamphlet, now very scarce, as having a 'tolerable share of beauty, and a majestic person'—qualities which certainly are more than borne out by the original portrait of her Grace, painted by Van Vost in 1711, and still to be seen at Drummond Castle. She has a magnificent high forehead, and prominent nose and chin: a mouth expressive of the most firm resolution; and brown eyes, a shade or two darker than her hair. As we look on that face, we can easily believe that her temper was 'rather imperious than soft,' and that she was as 'passionate' as 'obstinate.' We are told that even as a child she showed some traces of ferocity and cruelty; but, adds the writer (who, however, is prejudiced against her, as a 'female rebel'), 'since she commenced to play the warrior, she has given a full swing to the natural fierceness of her disposition, and in many cases has laid aside not only the woman, but even humanity.'

"It appears that when the Chevalier first landed

in the Highlands, the Duke of Perth, though
wishing well to his cause, was scarcely willing to
risk a rising in his favour; but his duchess, like a
true woman, was no such half-hearted partisan.
His Grace's disposition caused her great un-
easiness; 'she sweetened, cajoled, threatened, and
caressed him by turns; sometimes she was all
mildness, and would attempt to reason him into
her measures; at other times she was all fire and
flint, and would needs form him into her terms.
And when the Duke would reply, as he did sometimes, that he would gladly make an effort if he
saw a chance of success, she called him a 'poor
pusillanimous wretch,' and taunted him in bitter
terms with the meanness of waiting to see what
other chiefs would join the Chevalier's standard.
'You wait,' she cried, 'till some great man joins
him; another, till a third joins; and he till you
both join. The consequence will be that you will
be so long in debating as to whether it is safe to
join or not, that you will lose the opportunity for
ever. .... For God's sake! if you deserve to be
Duke of Perth, exert yourself suitably to your
rank, and show by your actions that you deserve
the title you bear by daring to fight for it.'"

In this way her Grace continued to urge the
Duke till Charles Edward was within a few miles
of Castle Drummond; and when her husband

would have gladly absented himself and washed his hands of the affair, she vowed that she would shut the gates against him and give him up as a prisoner to the Prince, if he would not stir himself. Accordingly, he thought it best to obey his spouse, and to wait on Charles Edward. So "he and she went in their coach and six, and met him about seven miles from Castle Drummond, where he lay that night." We can easily imagine with what zeal and politeness she exerted herself to entertain her royal guest, while the Duke sat by in a melancholy "brown study." Indeed so successfully did she ply her woman's weapons of banter, jest, and taunt, that before the Prince left the house the Duke had plucked up a spirit, and entered heart and soul into that brave but mad enterprise, which was to strip him of his princely possessions, and send him forth an exile and a wanderer, like the prince whose failing cause he espoused.

Next day the Duke contented himself with escorting the Prince as far as Perth, and with issuing a proclamation calling on his retainers to appear under the banner of the house of Castle Drummond within six days. But her Grace was a much more active partisan. She was out on horseback for three days and three nights, during which she never slept, and then returned to the castle at the head of seven hundred and fifty men. As the Duke had not come back, she set up the family standard with her own hand, proclaimed the Prince by the sound of bagpipes and hunting-horns, which she was obliged to use for want of trumpets, laid open her cellars to the multitude, and mounting on horseback, rode at the head of her troops to meet the Duke. The latter, who had no idea of seeing so many men under arms, was at first afraid, and thought that he was about to be seized and arrested; but the Duchess assured him there was no ground for alarm, and that the men at her back were her own levy. "The change of fancied enemies into real friends," says the pamphlet, "was very agreeable to the Duke and his party, who, it is said, showed very little stomach to fight, and if the joke had been carried any further, would in all probability have showed her Grace a pair of heels. This advantage afforded table talk to the young Pretender's court for a considerable time; and the banter was carried so far against the Duke that he was much annoyed at it, and the Pretender was obliged to put a stop to it by his authority.

Accompanying her husband and the Prince to Edinburgh, the Duchess added much to the brilliancy of his court at Holyrood. All sorts of anecdotes are told of her wit, her presence of mind, and readiness of resource. For instance, just before the Battle of Prestonpans, when her husband came to take leave of her in a desponding mood, she quietly said, " Well, you are going to the battle, and I to cards; both are in the hands of chance, and I shall be quite happy if you come back victorious, though with the loss of a leg or an arm; but I really care little whether you die on the field of honour or in my arms on a bed; but I would rather be the widow of a man who had died nobly in a righteous cause, than the wife of the greatest duke or prince on earth."

After the battle, she urged the Duke to follow up the success which he had thus far gained, and to push on while the enemy was panic-struck, before the King's troops could be brought together. But she seems to have been as cruel as she was audacious; for she urged her husband to put the prisoners that were taken to the sword, and to carry a Border castle by assault, or starve its holders into submission. And when she could not gain her point, it is recorded that she took a barbarous pleasure in insulting the prisoners whom she had in hand, and even blamed the Prince for treating them with common humanity.

When the Highland army crossed into England, the Duchess would not be left behind, but attended by only a lady friend, Mrs. Murray, and a single maid, she resolved to join in the campaign, though it was winter. In the March of that year she was up and on horseback with the daybreak; and when Carlisle surrendered, she strongly urged the policy of hanging all the townsmen, because they did not open their gates at her first summons, holding that it was a good thing to strike terror at once. Here, as is well known, both the Prince and her husband, not seeing much prospect of being able to carry the war by a *coup de main*, were inclined to turn back into Scotland; but her Grace set aside the idea by vowing that if her husband would not head the Drummonds, she would head them herself, and fight till not one remained; adding, with true female spite, that if he wished so much to save his pitiful carcass, she would try to do his part in the field, and he would not be much missed in the cabinet!

On the return of the army northwards, we are told that the citizens of Glasgow were made by her to feel the full weight of her resentment, and that it was through her that the levies and supplies enforced upon that city were so exorbitant. From this place, however, she found it necessary to return with the Duke and a detachment to Drummond Castle, and there she remained till the rest of the defeated Highlanders rejoined them. Here it would seem that, fairly brought to bay, and irritated to madness at the failure of her enterprise, she gave loose reins to her innate cruelty, not only taking a barbarous pleasure in seeing the common prisoners tortured, and insulting the officers, but showing herself a terror and scourge even to her own people. She was, we are told, so strict a disciplinarian that she would forgive no fault, however trifling, or neglect of her wishes even in trifles.

At Culloden her Grace was in the rear of the army, and it was with difficulty that she was prevented from appearing in the front. When the troops began to show some signs of rout, she saw a certain lord making away at full speed. As he passed her Grace, she cried out: "My Lord, you mistake your way: the enemies are behind, and you will not meet them in that direction!" In the retreat she helped to cover the hindmost of the fugitives, and wheeled round several times against the light horse that were in close pursuit. She kept with the fugitives as far as Inverness, where, worn out with vexation and disappointment far more than by actual fatigue, she was forced to rest for an hour, and there was arrested the same day, partly by force and partly by treachery, together with some other ladies of less note.

Long after her husband's death the Duchess continued, though passively, to maintain the Stuart cause in the North; and it is recorded of her that she had the greater part of the walls of Drummond Castle demolished and levelled to their foundations, in order to prevent it from being seized and garrisoned by the Royal troops. She remained there—so says the family tradition —until she saw the work of destruction completed, when she retired to Stobhall, in Perthshire, and there she ended her troubled days in peace at the age of about ninety years,

A fatality seems to have constantly followed the holders of the Ducal title. The Duke died at Paris in 1720, leaving two sons, James and John, both of whom, exiles in a foreign land, in turn assumed the coronet of barren strawberry leaves, though under attainder, while their noble estates were confiscated by the Crown, and given to the Drummonds of Lundin, a younger branch.

After John, the fourth duke, came two other dukes, his uncles; but they speedily followed each other to the tomb at St. Germain, issueless, and apparently unmarried. And in the year 1760 perished the last male descendant of the loyal Scottish Chancellor, the earldom being dormant, or presumed to have become extinct through the operation of the attainder thirty-five years previously.

A distant cousin, James Drummond, of Lundin, bent upon reviving, if possible, the lost but untarnished shield of the family, got himself served at Ediburgh in 1765 heir male of the exiled lords, and in consequence was recognised as head and representative of the house of Drummond. He was styled by his friends tenth Earl of Perth, and such no doubt, he was *de jure*, though the earldom was under the eclipse of the attainder. His son and successor, James, eleventh Earl, *de jure*, obtained in 1785 the restoration of the Drummond estates by the Court of Session and Act of Parliament, as being " the nearest collateral heir male of Lord John Drummond, in whom the lands had become forfeited in 1746." His Scottish earldom, however, was never recognised by the Crown or Parliament, nor did he ever attempt to record his vote at elections for Scottish representative peers. But in 1797, he was created a peer of Great Britain as Baron of Perth; he died, however, in 1800 without leaving a son; and the magnificent estates of the ancient Earls of Perth, including Drummond Castle, passed by inheritance to his only daughter and heir, who carried them in marriage to the Lord Willoughby de Eresby.

The representation, however, of the dormant earldom of Perth, apart from the possession of its *estates*, reverted to the nearest *heir male*, James Lewis, fourth Duke of Melfort in France (great grandson of John Drummond, Earl and Duke of Melfort.) He died, however, a few months subsequently, when his brother, Charles Edward Drummond, became fifth Duke of Melfort in France, and *de jure* thirteenth Earl of Perth in Scotland. Being a Catholic prelate, however, he was never able to effect the restoration of his dormant Scottish honours, or even to bring his case before the House of Lords. On his death at Rome, in 1840, the headship of the family devolved on his nephew, George Drummond, who was born in London in 1807, and for some years held a commission in the British Army. In 1853 his petition to that effect having been duly presented and considered, he was restored by the special command and recommendation of Her Majesty and by an Act of Parliament passed without a dissentient voice; and accordingly he is now fourteenth Earl of Perth in the peerage of Scotland, and sixth Duke of Melfort in France.

This dukedom is not a sham one, like that of the apocryphal and *soi-disant* "Duc de Roussillon," but a real and substantial title, regularly bestowed and regularly transmitted from its first grantee, John Drummond a grandson of the third Earl of Perth. Like his kinsman, Lord Perth followed King James to St. Germain, where on 17th April, 1692, he was raised to the dukedom by his sovereign, and the title was confirmed to him in France by *Le Grand Monarque*. He was, however, attainted in Scotland by the Parliament of that kingdom in 1695, expressly for having been seen at St. Germain.

Thus, for some six or seven generations have the ancient and loyal Drummonds been obliged to live as exiles from their native land, admitted to the courts of the Tuileries and Versailles, but banished from that of St. James's. Thus, under the stupid and senseless penal laws of the last century has Scottish energy, capacity, and integrity been added to the capital of France, and deducted from that of Great Britain, the loss of this country being precisely the gain of our neighbours. When the Drummonds fled into exile in 1688, *Le Grand Monarque* was graciously pleased to reward them not only with titles, but with a residence in the Royal Château at St. Germain, where they lived without intermission for a century or more; and I believe that I am not exceeding the liberty which has been allowed me when I add that Lady Clementina Davies, to whom I owe some of the intelligence contained in these pages, was the very last person born within the Château of St. Germain in October 1795, just before the necessities of the first French Revolution drove back the Drummonds to the shores which they had left for exile and comparative poverty in the cause of loyalty. *Aymez loyaulté,* is the motto of the Paulets, Marquisses of Winchester; but there is no need to write those words on the banners of the Drummonds, for they are already engraven upon their hearts. If not, they never will be now.

THE THREE MISS WALPOLES.

MY READERS no doubt will all remember the Miss Gunnings, the Court beauties about whom the whole fashionable world—indeed, I may say all the island from the Land's End to John o' Groat's House—ran mad some century and a quarter ago, and one of whom a contemporary writer styles the "Double Duchessed," in allusion to her having married two dukes in succession. Their story is somewhat strange in its way; but it is equalled, if not surpassed, in romance by the tale of the births, marriages, and ultimate fortunes of three beautiful Miss Walpoles, the daughters of Horace Walpole's brother Edward by a certain "left-handed" union, the details of which are to be seen in the "Memoirs of Horace Walpole and his Contemporaries," edited in 1845 by Eliot Warburton.

Sir Robert Walpole, who was for so many years Prime Minister under Kings George I. and II., and who was created Earl of Orford on retiring from public, or at all events ministerial, life, left three sons. The eldest was Robert, who succeeded as second earl; the youngest was Horace, the wit and antiquary of Strawberry Hill; and between them in the family tree stood the great stateman's second son Edward, (some time a Member of Parliament and Chief Secretary for Ireland), who, though he never himself wore a peer's coronet, became eventually the grandfather of one Royal Duke and of one Royal Princess, and the great-grandfather of at least one Duke and one Marquis in the Peerage of Great Britain.

Good looks were a heritage in the Walpole family. We are told that when the great Sir Robert Walpole was a young man about town he was one of the handsomest of a very handsome set; and a full share of his good looks appear to have passed to his son Edward, who was born in or about 1710. When he was only eighteen his appearance was so much in his favour that the ladies in Italy and Paris with one consent gave him the name of "the handsome Englishman." Having completed his education by going what was known as the "Grand Tour," without which no man of "quality" could be regarded as fit for society, he resolved to settle down in London, leading an easy, self-indulgent life as a bachelor, lodging at the West-end, and belonging to half a dozen clubs, where high play and Whig politics prevailed. In the year 1730 he occupied first-floor apartments over the shop of a certain tailor, in Pall Mall, named Rennie, who, we are told, made children's coats. As he passed daily by the shop, in order to get to his apartments, his notice was frequently attracted by one of the youthful apprentices—a fair girl with blue eyes and bright Saxon complexion—who worked in the shop, cutting out patterns and sewing small clothes. Her name was Mary Clement. Her family, though respectable, were too reduced in circumstances to give her any better education than such as she could pick up in Mr. Rennie's establishment; but though poor, they were anxious that she should maintain a good reputation. Mr. Edward Walpole somehow or other contrived to have frequent interviews with her when Rennie's back was turned, and to give her many little presents; but not so secretly as to escape the more penetrating eye of Mme. Rennie, who rated her soundly, and even sent for her father, in order to take her into the country out of the way of temptation. No doubt she lectured her pretty sharply on the great impropriety of her receiving presents and other attentions from so "fine" a gentleman as their lodger on the first floor, and tried hard to convince her how much more it would be to the advantage of "such a girl as plain Mary Clement to become the wife of a respectable tradesman in her own rank of life, rather than carry on a flirtation with one so much above her as Mr. Edward Walpole." Somehow or other, however, Mary Clement failed to see the matter from her mistress's point of view, though she appeared to be ready to listen to her disinterested advice, and even began to make ready for her departure. Indeed, it is said by one fussy chronicler of minute details that she "went upstairs and began to pack up her boxes," as apprentices and servant-girls usually do in such cases.

Be this, however, as it may, one thing is certain, namely, that the next morning, when Mr. Rennie opened his shop, there was no Mary Clement to be seen or found; and that as the day wore on she never returned to her needle. It appears that immediately on leaving Mrs. Rennie's presence she had rushed upstairs to the apartments of the "handsome Englishman; when"—to use the words of the biographer of the Walpoles— "he received her with open arms; she vowed that she would never leave him; and she kept her word." It is to be hoped, however, that Mr. Walpole, when he thus "received her with open arms," really meant only to wait for her father's death in order to give the poor girl who had thus thrown herself wholly on his honour, that position of a wife to which her beauty, her affection for him, and her then unsullied good name, conspired to entitle her.

By Mary Clement he had five children, two sons and three daughters; and it is due to his memory to add that he took every care which the fondest of fathers could take of their education. As children they were all remarkably handsome, like their parents. Her first boy appears to have died in childhood, having been probably carried off by the measles or the small-pox, which at that time claimed its annual tribute of victims from every house of "the upper ten thousand;" but of the three girls, as they grew up to womanhood, a contemporary writer of gossip avows his firm belief that, if the three Graces of the heathen poets returned to earth, it was doubtful whether they would be more afraid of the fair Walpoles or of the fair Gunnings (whom I have already mentioned) as rivals. After the birth of her fifth child, the poor devoted Mary Clement herself died, at the age of only four-and-twenty, her little son soon following her to the grave. Deep was the grief of the father of her children; and, although no plain gold ring had symbolised and blessed their union, he mourned her early death as any fond husband would have mourned the loss of the best and most affectionate of wives. But I must hasten on.

Mr. Edward Walpole was now not only a Member of Parliament, but the holder of more than one lucrative appointment under the Crown, and his father was in the zenith of his power as Prime Minister. Free from all the ties which the life of Mary Clement might have imposed upon him, still young and handsome, and with as brilliant prospects before him as any young man of his day, his position would have entitled him to think of marrying into any of the best families in the kingdom, with whom doubtless his three handsome daughters would not have been serious impediments: but he never would think or talk of marriage: his love was buried in the grave of Mary Clement, and his only thought was for his children. At all events, if at any time he entertained any ambitious desire of elevating himself, it was only with a view to their elevation that he coveted the distinction. He was installed a Knight of the Bath in 1753; and when the Duke of Devonshire became Lord-Lieutenant of Ireland,

Sir Edward Walpole was appointed Chief Secretary, and sworn a member of the Privy Council. He subsequently returned to England, and became Joint-Secretary of the Treasury—a post which no doubt he preferred to his splendid exile in Dublin, as it brought him back to that London life which he loved as well as did his brother Horace.*

The three daughters of Sir Edward were respectively named Laura, Maria, and Charlotte; they were elegant, lively, and highly accomplished, and of good temper and wit they had their full share. The portraits of Laura and Charlotte were painted in a single picture by Ramsay, and that of Maria by Sir Joshua Reynolds. At the Strawberry Hill sale these pictures fetched respectively fifty and seven hundred guineas. Indeed, they were already reckoned among the chief beauties of their time, and they excited the admiration of everyone who had the happiness of enjoying their society. Grand-daughters of the Prime Minister, and as amiable as they were lovely, they might fairly have appeared worthy of the affection of the proudest nobles of the land.

* It is said of Horace Walpole that he once whimsically declared at Strawberry Hill that he would like to be a doctor if only for one reason—that he might continually write for his patients one grand recipe for all complaints: "R. Haustus ccclxv. auræ Londin. in diem sumendos."

To any such idea, however, their left-handed birth opposed what—strange to say in a day when the King's German mistresses were raised wholesale to the peerage of England—appeared at the time an insuperable bar. They were known, not as Misses Clement, but by their father's name; but, by the prudish rules of St. James's they could not be presented at that Court where ladies by no means respectable were received wholesale; and so of course " those Miss Walpoles," as no doubt the Duchess of Kendal and Lady Walsingham snubbingly styled them, were never recognised by persons who could boast of an unsullied descent—so far as appears in the records of the Heralds' College.

On the other hand, Horace Walpole himself, be it said to his credit, was very partial to his brother's daughters, and constantly invited them to Strawberry Hill. Indeed, as might have been expected from one who combined as much as he did of the republican with the courtier, he was very proud of them one and all, notwithstanding the bend-sinister which marked their escutcheons, or, if I must speak heraldically, their " lozenges." His friends and correspondents record that he would gladly leave any of his favourite occupations, even his collections of old china, in order to attend upon his favourite nieces; and it was almost always a grand and festive day when the Lord of Strawberry Hill announced that he was to welcome the Walpole beauties within its Gothic walls. But there were also younger men than "Dear Uncle Horace," who were ready to leave their pursuits and professional studies in town in order to pass an afternoon in their charming society; and the lesser court of King Horace at Twickenham proved no contemptible rival to the greater court of King George and his Queen at St. James's.

In fact, the beauty and real goodness and worth of the Walpole girls conspired with the lax code of morality in the highest circles to break down the barriers which as yet stood in their way. Added to this, the prejudices which had hitherto kept members of aristocratic families from matching with young women of plain and untitled families were gradually passing out of date. Had not plain Sarah Jennings worn the ducal coronet of Marlborough, and ruled as a queen of society, even over kings and queens and courts? And were the grand-daughters of Sir Robert Walpole, though not born in wedlock, to be debarred from the outer circle of a court where even the marriage of a lady was no guarantee of her correct conduct?

The first young man of good birth and high

prospects—be it said to his credit—who resolved to set this code at defiance, was the Hon. and Rev. Frederick Keppel, a younger brother of the Earl of Albemarle. He was a clergyman of good character and fair position, already holding preferment in the Established Church, and one who not unreasonably might look forward to the prospect of further promotion. He much admired Laura, the eldest of the three, and he thought he saw in her those qualities which would make a good wife for a clergyman. He knew the history of Mary Clement, and in spite of it he resolved to propose for her daughter. Horace Walpole thus writes on the subject:

"I have forgot to tell you of a wedding in our family; my brother's eldest daughter is to be married to-morrow to Lord Albemarle's brother, a canon of Windsor. We are very happy with the match. The bride is very agreeable, sensible, and good, though not so handsome, perhaps, as her sisters. . . . The second, Maria, is beauty itself. Her face, bloom, eyes, hair, teeth, and person are all perfect. You may image how charming she is when I tell you that her only fault, if one must find one, is that her face is rather too round. She has a great deal of wit and vivacity, with perfect modesty."

Mr. Keppel, already canon of Windsor, my

readers may be glad to learn, lived to mount the ladder of further promotion, and died Bishop of Exeter; nor did I ever hear that he found cause to regret the choice that he made when he married the daughter of plain Mary Clement. As the untitled daughter of that untitled lady, the doors of St. James's had been closed against her; but as " the Hon. Mrs Keppel" she at once appeared at court, and was duly presented to the King and Queen "on her marriage," as is written in the book of the chronicles of the *Court Circular* of the day.

It is needless to state that after this marriage of the elder sister, the chances in favour of the beautiful Maria and of Charlotte making " good matches" increased wonderfully, and that they soon found as good a market to carry their matrimonial wares to as they could have found at the " drawing-room " of royalty. In fact, the sisters-in-law of the Keppels appear to have been sisters-in-love as well as sisters-in-law; and in general society the prejudices which for a time had stood in the way of the young ladies' advancement soon began to crumble away. Introduced into general society by the Keppels, they were received everywhere among the Suffolk county families, Maria, the beauty of the family, creating a marked sensation wherever she appeared.

Among the numerous admirers of the belle of the season was a certain noble earl, of high and noble descent, who, though not quite young, nor yet quite advanced in years, thought himself not too old to take a young wife. Maria Walpole, he thought, was by far the most lovely woman that he had ever seen, at all events that he knew; but then it was the old story, "There were objections," strong, though possibly not insurmountable. His lordship, who was no other than James, second Earl Waldegrave, had held the highly respectable post of Governor and Privy Purse to the Prince of Wales; he was also Privy Councillor, a Knight of the Garter, and a Teller of the Exchequer; and it would scarcely be becoming, he thought, to fly in the face of his royal master, and offend courtly propriety by marrying a lady whom the King and Queen could not possibly recognise, even though that lady was a Walpole. But while Lord Waldegrave was striving to digest his scruples, and to weigh his interest against his inclinations, he found the prize within his reach was daily becoming more and more precious in the eyes of several persons of distinction who had similar opportunities with himself of observing how much more lustre the matchless face of Maria Walpole would add to a coronet than a coronet would add to her face. The earl also could not but remember that he was already four-and-forty, and that there were plenty of younger rivals in the field who would be likely to take advantage of any indecision on his part. Indeed he was given to understand by one of those kind lady friends who love to have a finger in the pie of every match-making arrangement, that with his lordship it was a question of "now or never," and it was no season for shilly-shallying.

The result was, as might have been expected, that the Prince's Governor and Privy Purse, Earl, Privy Councillor, Knight of the Garter, and Teller of the Exchequer though he was, came to a decision to follow the example of Mr. Keppel, and lay his honours and coronet at the feet of the daughter of the poor tailor's apprentice. Accordingly, in the year 1759, Maria Walpole became Countess Waldegrave, and, like her elder sister, was duly "presented at Court." Lord Waldegrave, it may be remarked, had some pretensions to unite himself with so intellectual and literary a family as the Walpoles, as being one of the "noble authors" of his day. He had composed a volume of "Historical Memoirs," extending from 1754 to 1758; a work with respect to which it is remarked with some *naïveté* by Mr. Eliot Warburton, that "it is true he was the historian of rather a short period; but then it must be remembered that in four years much may be done, and, therefore much may be written about it." His lordship, I believe, never found reason to regret his choice; and he had three daughters by his countess, who proved as good a mother as wife. Four years after her marriage, and just after the birth of her last child, the Earl was struck with the small-pox, of which he died. She nursed him, however, through his illness with all care and affection, and regardless of all consequences to herself, as I learn on the testimony of her uncle Horace; and she deeply lamented his loss; indeed, for many a long month she was inconsolable. To her own prospects, apparently, the loss of Lord Waldegrave was a severe blow, as only a few days before his last illness he had been offered the choice of two splendid appointments—the Ambassadorship at Paris or the Lord-Lieutenancy of Ireland.

It was long before the widowed countess would venture again into society; but society felt that it had a claim upon her, and was not slow to enforce its claim. More lovely than ever on her reappearance in fashionable circles, the youthful widow drew on herself more admiring eyes, if possible, than she had done in her early maiden days. Her three little girls engrossed all her attentions and affections. Many of the first and highest nobles in the land sought to share their honours and possessions with the charming relict; but the Countess was obdurate, and a long train of rejected suitors, with the Duke of Portland at their head, passed away from her doors.

But the whirligig of time brings round its revenges. A few years of widowhood passed by when another pretender to the widow's hand entered the field, and the very lady against whom only seven brief years before the doors of "our Palace of St. James's were closed and barred was now sought in marriage by the King's own brother. "A singular union indeed," as Mr Eliot Warburton remarks, "of the two extreme links of the social chain took place when H.R.H. William Henry, Duke of Gloucester, in 1766, espoused the daughter of the unfortunate Mary Clement—a marriage in virtue of which it was not only possible*, but quite probable, that a descendant of the tailor's apprentice might in course of time take his or her seat upon that very throne to which her own daughters had been denied all approach." The issue of this second marriage was (1) a son, Prince William Frederick, Duke

---

* What is known as the Royal Marriage Act, passed at the instance of George III., was one of the consequences of this union.

of Gloucester, who married the Princess Mary, daughter of King George III., and died in 1834; and (2) a daughter, the Princess Sophia, who died unmarried in 1844. It may be interesting here to record the fact that Maria's three little girls by her first husband all lived to grow up and married well; the eldest becoming the wife of her cousin George, fourth Earl Waldegrave, and eventually the owner of Strawberry Hill; the second marrying George Henry, fourth Duke of Grafton; while the third married Admiral Lord Hugh Seymour, the grandfather of the present Marquis of Hertford.

And do my readers wish to know the matrimonial fate of Charlotte, the youngest of the three of the Walpole beauties? She was married in 1760 to Lionel, Lord Huntingtower, afterwards fourth Earl of Dysart in the Scottish peerage. But they shall hear the story in the words of her uncle Horace. He writes under date Oct. 2, 1760:

"I announce to you my Lady Huntingtower. I hope you will approve the match . . . . I suppose my Lord Dysart will, as he does not yet know, though they have been married these two hours, that at ten o'clock this morning his son married my niece Charlotte at St. James's Church. The moment my Lord Dysart is dead, I will carry you to see Ham House. It is pleasant to call neighbours cousins, with a charming prospect over against one. And now, if you want to know the detail, there was none. It is not the style of our little court to have long negotiations; and we do not fatigue the town with exhibiting the betrothed parties for six months together in public places. *Venit, vidit, vicit.* The young lord has liked her for some time; on Saturday sen'night he came to my brother and made his demand. The princess did not know him by sight, and did not dislike him when she did; she consented, and they were to be married this morning: My Lord Dysart is such a fool that nobody will pity him. He has kept his son till six and twenty, and would never make the least settlement on him. "Sure," said the young man, "if my father will do nothing for me, I may please myself; he cannot hinder me of £10,000 a year, and £60,000 more that are in the funds, all entailed on me on a reversion," which one does not wonder that the bride did not refuse, as there is present possession too of a very handsome person, the only thing his father has ever given him."

"In another letter the chatty and communicative old uncle thus tells the story in its full details, which are too amusing to be lost to my readers:

"My brother's last daughter, Charlotte, is

married, and . . . . . though their story is too short for a romance, it will make a very pretty novel; nay, it is almost brief enough for a play, coming very nearly within one of the unities, the space of twenty-four hours. There is in the world . . . . and he lives directly over against me, across the water, a strange brute called the the Earl of Dysart. Don't be frightened, he is not the bridegroom. His son, Lord Huntingtower, to whom he gives but £400 a year, is a comely young gentleman of six-and-twenty, who has often had thoughts of trying whether his father would not like grandchildren better than he does his own children. . . . . All the answer he could ever get was that, as he had five younger children, the Earl could not afford to make any settlement; but he offered, as a proof at once of his inability and his kindness, to *lend* his son a large sum of money at a low interest. This indigent earl has thirteen thousand a year and sixty thousand pounds in the funds. This money, and ten out of the thirteen thousand, are entailed upon Lord Huntingtower. The young Lord, it appears, had been in love with Charlotte for some months, but thought so little of inflaming her that yesterday fortnight she did not know him by sight. On that day he proposed himself as a son-in-law to my brother, who with much surprise heard his story, but excused himself from giving an answer. He said he would never force the inclinations of his children; he did not believe his daughter Charlotte had any engagement or attachment, but she might have; he would send for her and know her mind. She was with her sister Maria, to whom she said very sensibly, 'If I were but nineteen, I would refuse point blank, for I don't like to be married in a week to a man I never saw. But I am two-and-twenty. Some people say I am handsome, and some say I am not; but I believe the truth is that I am likely to be at large and to go off soon. It is dangerous to refuse so great a match.' Take notice of the words 'married in a week.' The love that was so many months in ripening could not stay above a week. She came and saw the impetuous lover, and I believe she was glad that she had not " refused point blank," for they were married last Thursday. I tremble a little for the poor girl; not to mention the oddness of the father and twenty disagreeable things that may be in the young man, who has been kept and has lived entirely out of the world. He takes her fortune, and cannot settle another shilling upon her till his father dies, and then promises only a thousand a year. Would one venture one's happiness, and one's whole fortune too, for the chance of living to be Lady Dysart? If Lord Huntingtower dies before his father she will not have a sixpence. Surely my brother has risked too much!"

In a letter of subsequent date the gossiping old uncle follows up the subject with a story too good to be omitted here:

"Lord Huntingtower wrote to offer his father eight thousand pounds of Charlotte's fortune if he would give them a thousand a year at present and settle a jointure on her. The Earl returned this truly laconic . . . . answer: 'Lord Huntingtower.—Sir, I answer your letter as soon as I receive it. I wish you joy. I hear your wife is very accomplished.—Yours, DYSART.'

"I believe my Lady Huntingtower must make it convenient that Lord Dysart should die, and then he will. For myself, I expect to be a very respectable personage in time, and to have my tomb set forth like the Lady Margaret Douglas, that I had four earls for my nephews, though I never was one myself. Adieu."

The "strange brute" of an earl died in 1770, and Charlotte Lady Huntingtower thereon became Countess of Dysart. She died, however, issueless. Horace Walpole's prophecy, however, was never quite fulfilled; it is true that his nephew, George, a queer, eccentric, and half-cracked creature, became third Earl of Orford, and that two of his three nieces wore the coronets of countesses, namely, those of Waldegrave and Dysart; but Maria was obliged to be content with seeing her husband hold a spiritual peerage, which gave no coronet to herself. Horace Walpole, however, made up for this deficiency in two ways; first by his second niece becoming a princess of the blood royal, and secondly by succeeding, though late in life, to his nephew's earldom, a title which became extinct at his death, though revived subsequently in another branch of the family.

In conclusion, I must add that Sir Edward Walpole's only son, Edward, the brother of the beauties whose stories I have attempted to tell, entered the army, and distinguished himself while a subaltern by an act of gallantry which will be found duly recorded in the Walpole Letters. His name is not mentioned in the "Peerages" along with those of his sisters; but it is satisfactory to know that he rose to the rank of lieutenant-colonel. Of his ultimate fate I have been able to learn nothing.

THE WOOING OF SIR HENEAGE FINCH.*

THE name of Heneage Finch is one which for nearly two centuries has held a foremost place both in the pages of the peerage, and also among those Englishmen who have gained distinction as " learned in the law," or as leaders in affairs of state. Every Earl of Aylesford in succession, from the first peer, who was Chancellor of the Duchy of Lancaster in the reign of George I., down to the present holder of the title, representing no less than seven generations, has borne that name; and the first Lord Aylesford himself was the distinguished son of an even more distinguished father, Heneage Finch, who, having been one of the

* It may be desirable to state that this was written before I had seen an article on the same subject in *Temple Bar* for July, 1872.

leading members of the Parliament which restored King Charles II., became successively Solicitor and Attorney-General, Lord Keeper of the Great Seal, and ultimately was advanced to the woolsack and created Earl of Nottingham. This Sir Heneage Finch, while in the prime of manhood, was not only Treasurer of the Inner Temple, but also " Autumn or Summer Reader" of that society, and in that capacity he gained a high reputation for his practical and common-sense application of the general principles of the law—a subject which as yet had not been taken in hand by Judge Blackstone. His "readings" in the Temple, we are told, were very popular and quite the fashion of the day: so that we must not be surprised to find that they were attended by many members of other professions and the wits and courtiers of the second Charles; and that he brought them to a conclusion by a grand entertainment which he gave to the King and his Court in the great hall of the Temple, where a play or 'masque' was performed by the students in the presence of his Majesty.

But if we go yet another generation back, we shall find that this Lord Chancellor's father was also a Sir Heneage Finch, and a man of some note in his day—at all events, he was serjeant-at-law, Recorder of London, and Speaker of the House of Commons under King Charles I. in 1626.

It is this Sir Heneage Finch the story of whose second wooing I propose to tell. By his first wife, a daughter of Sir Edmund Bell, of Beaupré Hall, Norfolk, he had a family of seven sons and four daughters, so that he must have been well forward in years—or at all events, as they say, no chicken—when he first set his eyes on a rich and charming widow, one Mistress Elizabeth Bennett, the daughter of a Staffordshire gentleman named Cradock, and whom the recent death of her husband, Richard Bennett, a citizen of London, and a parishioner of St. Olave's, Jewry, had left at her own disposal, together with a good round sum of money and other property.

By the custom of London, and by the will of her departed lord, it appears that she was in actual possession of two-thirds of her husband's goods and chattels, besides jewels and chains of pearl and gold, and some splendid diamond and other rings, to say nothing of the family plate, the family coach, with four "grey coach mares and geldings," and other good things to boot. In addition to these substantial recommendations, she seems to have had no small share of personal attractions—with a full consciousness of their value, no doubt—and no more drawbacks and incumbrance than one little boy. In those days, although the "Duke of Roussillon" was not born or thought of, it was scarcely necessary for a pretty widow to advertise for a husband; and the fair Mistress Bennett accordingly had no lack of suitors for her hand and heart.

Much to the amusement of the wits who moved about in London society at that time, three of the most conspicuous among the rival candidates bore the names of birds—Sir Sackville Crow, a physician named Raven, and the Sir Heneage Finch whom we have already introduced to our readers; and besides these we have on record a fourth suitor, Sir Edward Dering, of Surrenden Dering, in Kent, and sundry other titled and untitled individuals, whose names we shall have occasion to mention presently.

The course of true love, in the case of Sir Heneage, appears to have given the lie to the old proverb by "running" tolerably "smoothly." It is true that he had no lack of rivals; and, though it might be supposed that the chances were in favour of a man, like himself, who had filled the Speaker's chair, and must therefore have been of courtly and commanding presence, and who had the still more substantial endowments of a town house, and also an estate and mansion at

Kensington,* with high Court connections to boot, yet for several months it seemed as if he was not unlikely to be distanced in the race by one of the aforesaid birds, and still more by the Kentish squire, Sir Edward Dering, whose efforts to win the hand and heart of the pretty widow were equally artful and persistent. It is from one of the old manuscripts preserved among the archives of Surrenden Dering, and given to the world under the auspices of the Camden Society,† that I may gather such information on the subject as I am enabled to lay before my readers.

The lady's first husband had died only in the April of 1628, but by the end of that year she was already besieged by a host of worshippers, all more or less bent, we may believe, on securing a share of her money;

"Juventus
Non tantum veneris quantum studiosa culinæ;"

for it was publicly reported at the time that she was "a twenty thousand pound widow." The

---

* The house is said to have stood very nearly on the site now occupied by Kensington Palace, and part of Kensington Palace Gardens formed part of Sir H. Finch's landed estate.

† Proceedings in the County of Kent; from certain MSS. in the possession of Sir E. Dering, Bart., at Surrender Dering. Edited by the Rev. L. B. Larking; published by the Cambridge Camden Society, 1862.

first bird who flew citywards to find her out was apparently a wise specimen of his kind; at all events, Sir Sackville Crow, for such was his title, was making a desperate effort at that time to relieve himself from the consequences of a serious deficit in his public accounts, which shortly afterwards compelled him to retire from his office of Treasurer of the Navy. He came, he saw, he proposed, and he did *not* conquer. The widow, though amorously inclined, was not to be easily caught; he had to return to his nest discomfited, and we do not hear of him again eastwards of Temple Bar.

The next person who tried his luck with the widow was determined not to be so easily baffled, and accordingly resolved to take her literally by assault. This was Dr. Raven, a fashionable and successful physician of the day. In despair of other and gentler means, this foolish man thought that Mrs. Bennett could be won by a *coup de main*, if the bold stroke could be made with sufficient vigour. Accordingly, by tampering with her servants, so as to silence her personal attendant or get her out of the way, he made his entry into the lady's chamber after she had retired to rest on the 19th of November, in the year already mentioned. His reception was such as might have been imagined. The lady screamed

"Thieves!" and "Murder!" so as to be heard by the "Charleys" in Cheapside; the servants, male and female, rushed to the rescue; the doctor was secured, and handed over to the constable, who next day brought the intruder before "Mr. Recorder." As Mr. Recorder—in other words, Sir Heneage Finch—was himself one of the rival suitors for the lady's hand, we may imagine the pleasure with which he signed the order for committing Dr. Raven to durance vile until he could be brought to trial. The Court refused to allow him to be bailed. He was ultimately tried, fined, and imprisoned for the affair; but the loss of his professional guineas no doubt was a still severer penalty.

On the next day Sir Edward Dering, as he tells us, was in the field. His tale is told with much *naïveté*, and shows us that servants were as accessible to golden arguments as they were in the days of Jupiter and Danaë, or as they can be now. "Nov. 20, Edmund the King. I adventured, but was denied. Sent up a letter, which was returned after she had read it."

This repulse rendered it necessary to resort to other, and we fear that we must add crooked, means. Servants are amenable to bribes; and accordingly Sir Edmund's diary continues: "Nov. 21. I inveigled G. Newman with 20s.—Nov.

24. I did re-engage him (20s). I did also oil the cash keeper (20s).—Nov. 26. I gave Edmund Aspull (the cash keeper) another 20s."

This looks unpromising, but it appears as if Sir Edward did not readily lose courage along with his cash. The next entry, consequently, shows a faint glimmer of hope: "Nov. 27. I sent a second letter, *which was* kept."

But in spite of his rising hopes, the worthy knight feels that he must not relax his efforts. Accordingly he writes, the same day: "I set Sir John Skeffington upon Matthew Cradock."

This Matthew, we may remark, was a cousin of the widow, and her trusty adviser in matters of business. The diary continues, under the same day's date: "The cash keeper supped with me."

Neither Sir John Skeffington, however, nor the "cash keeper" appears to have been of much practical use, or possibly they did not do their best on his behalf. Accordingly Sir Edward begins to act seriously for himself: "Nov. 30. I was at the Old Jewry Church, and saw her, both forenoon and afternoon. Dec. 1. I sent her a third letter, which was likewise kept."

On the following Sunday Sir Edward, "true to his tryste," went to St. Olave's, when, on coming out of church, George Newman whispered in his ear, "Good news, good news!" Sir Edward who had taken a lodging in sight of the widow's house, pressed his informant to come in. George Newman—the same who had been "inveigled" and "oiled"—quietly and confidentially told Sir Edward that his lady "liked well his carriage, and that if his lands were not already settled on his eldest son, there was good hope for him." The bearer of such good news certainly deserved a repetition of the oiling process, and accordingly, says Sir Edward, "I gladly gave him another twenty shillings."

Elated and hopeful, Sir Edward, in the course of the evening, proceeded to call on the Recorder. Sir Edward, being a man of Kent, very naturally stayed to supper, and as naturally grew very confidential as he drank the worthy knight's wine. Sir Heneage, too, grew confidential in his turn, gave him to understand that he quite despaired of success himself, and, indeed, meant gradually and quietly to withdraw; in fact, he went so far as to promise his aid to Sir Edward's cause. So in the course of the evening the two suitors frankly and freely chatted over the widow and her affairs, and the Recorder put Sir Edward wholly off his guard. Good easy Kentish baronet! you are no match for a lawyer like Sir Heneage Finch, let alone a wily and wary widow, whose choice in the matter is well known to him, as he carries the game in his hands.

It so happened that one great obstacle in the way of the widow's remarriage was the wardship of her little boy, which belonged to a certain Mr. Steward, but which he was willing to relinquish for a money payment. The widow offered what she (and Sir Heneage too) thought a fair sum; but he refused, and raised his price to so extortionate an amount that the widow refused to see him or speak to him again.

Sir Edward thought that this was the juncture to push his suit. It appears from the narrative that for a few days the lady, like many others, did not quite know her own mind, and would neither say 'yes' nor 'no;' so, weary of waiting, on the 1st of January he wrote and demanded the return of his letters and *billets-doux*. His cause was now irretrievably lost; for, in spite of all arguments and recommendations in his favour from the lady's "companion," Mrs. Norton, and his friend, the celebrated angler and man-milliner of Fleet-street, Izaak Walton, and the clever machinery of some dreams, real or fictitious, which were told to the lady in one of her softer moods by cousins and friends of the baronet, and the (of course) accidental waylaying of her

little boy and his nurse in the fields of Finsbury
and plying them with cakes, wine, and money,
the widow stood to her guns, and positively
refused to think of him any more as a suitor. In
fact (so she gave it out), she never meant to
marry again at all. Suitors came and went.
Great ladies from the Court—the cream of
"carriage folk"—visited the mansion in St.
Olave's in shoals, and set forth the merits of
sundry knights and gentlemen and lords, but all
without effect. Lady Skinner called to plead
the cause of one Mr. Butler; but her description
of him as a "dark, blunt-nosed gentleman"
extinguished his hopes and ended his suit. Sir
Peter Temple, of Stowe, a man of high birth,
and the owner of lands which have since enriched
the ducal house of Buckingham, came forward,
backed by the aid of a dashing countess, but
found only a cold reception, being told to go
back to Buckinghamshire. The Countess of
Bridgwater introduced the battered old sailor Sir
Henry Mainwaring, who, in spite of his Cheshire
pedigree, was steeped in poverty to the very lips,
and he and another knight had an interview of an
hour with the lady, but neither of them was
suffered to call again. Lord Bruce—the head
of the Bruces of Tottenham, now Earls and
Marquises of Ailesbury—put in a claim for

himself; but he too very soon retired. More persevering than the rest of the candidates for this very prudent Penelope, and, indeed, the only dangerous rival of Sir Heneage, was the newly-made Lord Lumley, whose chances were all the better as he came backed by one Loe, or Lowe, a brother-in-law of the lady herself.

The latter, it must be owned, lost no opportunity of prosecuting his suit by overt attentions to the widow. As being one of "the devout female sex," it appears she went to daily prayers at St. Olave's Church; and accordingly five times in one week did the coach of Lord Lumley stop the way at the door of the church in Old Jewry, its owner being intent on worshipping there, though possibly the rich widow may have been one object of his worship. His suit was backed by no less a person than the Earl of Dorset, Lord Chamberlain to the Queen, an influential person in the political world, and especially at the Admiralty. But all was in vain; weeks and weeks drew on, yet the lady was still obdurate; she would not listen, she said, to any proposal of matrimony; her mind had been long made up. Isaak Walton now again appears upon the scene, to plead once more the cause of his old friend, Sir Edward; but her answer was the same. Lord Lumley had even proceeded so far at one time as to present her with a ring, which she accepted at his hands; but it was not a plain gold one, and on the 14th of February his hopes were crushed by the return of the pledge of attachment.

And so it was: the widow all along, at all events from the preceding Christmas, *had made up her own mind;* but, like most rich and pretty widows, not at all in the direction of a life-long celibacy. She did not use the deepest of black-bordered note paper, or mount a long flowing white widow's cap on a rope of black silk, talk of herself as a "wreck," and of her life as a *vie manquée*, and carry on private flirtations in a dark room with charlatans and adventurers. But she kept her own counsel, and had her own way in the end; and having contrived to delude Sir Edward into an idea that the resumption of his place as a suitor was not absolutely a fruitless and hopeless task, one fine morning she surprised both him and the fashionable world, and everybody else except the worthy Recorder of London, by going quietly on the 16th of April, 1629— after exactly twelve months of widowhood—to the Church of St. Clement Danes, where she was married, no doubt by special licence, to Sir Heneage Finch, with whom the affair no doubt had been pre-arranged ever since the previous

Christmas. It may interest our lady friends to learn that Sir Edward Dering took his defeat in good part, and soon set about retrieving his lost ground, time, and trouble by electing as his third wife — he had already buried two — a daughter of Sir Ralph Gibbes, of Honington, Warwickshire, with whom, no doubt, he "lived happy ever afterwards."

Before we dismiss our notice of the pretty widow, it may be well to add that her son Simon — whom Sir Edward Dering treated with cakes in Finsbury Fields — became in the end a man of great wealth, which was carried by three daughters, his coheiresses, into several noble families, and that his uncle, Richard Bennett, or Bennet as the name is now spelt, was the ancestor of the Earls of Arlington and Tankerville. Of Mrs. Bennett's second mariage all that we know is bright and fortunate, except its brief continuance; and it is probable that among the many suitors, both bachelors and widowers, who sought her hand, she really chose the best, or one of the best. Of the issue of Sir Heneage Finch's first marriage, three sons and one daughter lived to grow up; and the eldest of these, named as his father, became Lord Chancellor of England and Earl of Nottingham, a title with which his descendants and representatives have joined the

Earldom of Winchelsea. By the pretty and wealthy widow, Sir Heneage had two daughters, Elizabeth, wife of Edward Maddison, Esq., and Anne, married to Edward, third Viscount and first Earl of Conway, ancestor of the present Marquis of Hertford. Sir Heneage Finch survived his marriage little more than two years, as he died on the 5th of December, 1631.

THE DUCAL HOUSE OF LEEDS.

OUT of all the great families who have attained to the honour of a ducal coronet in England, most owe their existence either to the accident of being sprung from royalty by a left-hand marriage, or from successful statesmanship subsidised by a run of luck in the way of alliances with well-endowed heiresses. Some few dukedoms, I am aware—those of Wellington and Marlborough, for instance — have been purchased by a series of brilliant achievements in the field; one, and one only so far as I know —that of Norfolk—is sprung out of the successful career of an able lawyer; but there is one house, namely, that of the Osbornes, Dukes of Leeds, in whose early history is to be found an episode of city life so strange and so singular that I need scarcely ask the pardon of my readers for introducing it to them here.

The romance to which I allude is nearly three centuries old, though it reads like an affair of yesterday. But before I come to tell it, I will beg my readers' patience while I sum up in a few words all that is known of the earlier history of the Osborne family. It is agreed among the heralds and the peerage makers that the Osbornes were of considerable antiquity in Kent long before they attained to the honours of the peerage, or even to a title at all. We are told that one John Osborne, esquire and landholder, was seated at Ashford in that county as far back as the reign of King Henry VI., when his name is returned in a list of the local gentry, as subscribing to the oath of allegiance. His lineal descendant, Richard Osborne, married a Kentish lady, Elizabeth Fylden or (more probably) Tylden; and *his* son, also Richard, marrying a Broughton of Westmorland, became the father of a certain Edward Osborne, who, entering early upon a commercial life, served as one of the Sheriffs of London and Middlesex in the seventeenth year of Elizabeth's reign, and eight years later was chosen in due course Lord Mayor of London. He received the honour of knighthood at Westminster in 1584, and not long afterwards was chosen one of the representatives of the City of London in Parliament. He died in the year 1591, and was buried in the church of St. Dionis Backchurch, where a monument recorded, and perhaps still records, his public and private virtues. Collins, in his elaborate "Peerage," simply says of him that "he married Anne, daughter and heiress of Sir William Hewitt, also in his time Lord Mayor of London," adding incidentally also that "Sir William died in the year 1566, when his said daughter, Anne, was just twenty-three years of age."

Sir William Hewitt appears to have been a charitable and benevolent person. He was a benefactor to several of the hospitals of London, and to the poor of more than one parish. Thus he left to the poor in the hospital of St. Thomas's, Southwark (of which he was a vice-president), £20; and 4s. 8d. to every poor maiden that should be married within a year of his decease in two parishes in Yorkshire, with which it may be presumed that he was connected by family ties. The disposal of the rest of his property is already incidentally recorded in the present paper. By his will, dated Jan. 3, 1566, I find he ordered his body to be buried in the church of St. Martin's, in Candlewick Ward (of which he was a parishioner), near to the place where his late beloved wife Alice was interred.

But, for the sake of my lady readers, I must not pass quite so rapidly over a marriage out of which such important consequences flowed to the Osbornes. Respectable and even ancient as the family might have been at Ashford, in Kent, it is pretty clear that they must have suffered severely in purse and pocket when, in the reign of Mary or of Elizabeth, Richard Osborne sent his eldest son, no doubt the eldest of a large family—up to London to fight for himself the battle of life. And doubtless either a special Providence or a very lucky star looked down with more than a kind smile on young Edward Osborne, when the latter, at the age of eighteen or nineteen summers, reached London from Ashford, and entered the family of Sir William Hewitt and of Dame Alice Hewitt, of Philpot Lane, as an "apprentice" to learn his trade. At that time youthful apprentices were not left to pass their time in suburban lodgings, walking backwards and forwards to their daily work, and when the day's task was over, enlivening their evenings at theatres and music halls. When they were bound as apprentices, they became inmates of their master's household, and were expected, as members of his family, to conform

to the rules and regulations of the homes of which
which they formed a part. Of course, if their
masters happened to have grown-up or growing
daughters, the young fellows had so many more
attractions to keep them at home and out of
mischief; and equally of course was it a matter
of constant occurrence that the best and the
worthiest of such apprentices were enabled to
climb the first rung of the ladder of commercial
advancement by securing the affections of one of
the pretty and well-endowed daughters of their
master. And it was only the old old story after
all that was enacted in the family of Sir William
Hewitt, that I have to tell. It appears that,
having no other incumbrance but his daughter,
and having made a fair fortune in business, Sir
William and Lady Hewitt, with "Mistress"
Anne and their Kentish apprentice, had removed
from the worthy knight's place of business in
Philpot Lane, and were occupying a fashionable
residence on old London Bridge, every arch of
which, as shown in old pictures, was at that time
crowded with houses. The windows on one side
at least looked down upon the never-ceasing ebb
and flow of the Thames; and, as bad (or good)
luck would have it, one day while fair Mistress
Anne was hanging her favourite bird in its cage
outside the parlour window, she lost her balance

and fell out into the river. It was fortunately just high water, so that she had not many feet to fall, and the tide was running very slackly; but the river was deep, and in a few minutes more she would have been drowned, had not the young gentleman from Kent, who counted swimming among the other accomplishments which he had learned at his native Ashford, thrown off his shoes and surcoat, and leaped into the water after her. It was the work of an instant. He caught by her hair the struggling maiden, and dragged her towards a barge which was passing through the bridge; the crew hove to, and took on board the half-drowned lady and her preserver; and the latter being landed at the steps between the bridge and Fish-street-hill, brought back his prize with no small joy and triumph to her father's house, where doubtless every attention was paid to them both. It was fortunately Summer, and so they both escaped with no further bad results than a sound ducking, and possibly a slight cold.

Perhaps it was scarcely *à priori* probable that the matter would end there. Mistress Anne, as I have reason for believing, had long secretly admired the young gentleman of good family from Kent, who had been for so many months an inmate of her parents' house, and who in all matters, great and small, had shown himself a thorough gentleman in deed as he was by birth. He shot well with the long bow, whenever the young apprentices of the city went out to what is now Moorfields and Clerkenwell in order to try their skill. In Winter time he was the best skater and curler among all the city-youths; he could sing a loyal song with spirit; and was always in the best of tempers. In fact, if the truth must be told, she admired him above all the young men whom she had seen east of what is now Temple Bar; and into the far western region of the mansions of the Strand and of Westminster it had not been her fortune to have often entered, except on one day in the year when she went regularly with her papa and mamma in the family coach to visit an old aunt at St. Giles-in-the-Fields, "from whom she had expectations."

Edward Osborne also had long admired in silence the young lady whose cage-bird had given rise to this unexpected adventure, and the keen eyes of Dame Alice Hewitt had not been inattentive to the fact. The old people too were rich and without a son. What arrangement more simple, obvious, and easy than that Edward Osborne should become their son-in-law? The young people, for their part, took the same view of the matter as their elders; interest and inclination for once ran in the same direction; and within a fortnight from the day of the apprentice's bold leap into the Thames it was arranged that the banns of " Edward Osborne, bachelor, and Anne Hewitt, spinster," should be put up in their parish church.

As neither Sir William nor Dame Hewitt was at all disposed to forbid the banns, everything was soon settled; and one fine morning in August, 1559, the church bells of St. Magnus and the neighbouring parishes rang out a merry peal in honour of Edward Osborne and his fair young bride.

Sir William Hewitt, before his death, which happened at no very distant date, constituted his son-in-law Osborne executor of his will, along with two members of his own family; and while he left to his brother and nephews the place of business in Philpot Lane above mentioned, he bequeathed the bulk of his money to his only child Anne Hewitt, now Anne Osborne.

The accession of the money of the Hewitts to the exchequer of the Osbornes appears to have come just at a favourable moment, and to have given to that ancient house a chance of rising in the world—a change of which its members were not slow to take advantage. Edward Osborne was wise enough not to play the fine-gentleman, or to turn his back upon the city where his fortune had been and was still being made. He persevered in the mercantile career which he had chosen when a lad, and he resolved to stick to it faithfully to the last. Accordingly we find him filling the civic chair as Lord Mayor and receiving the honour of knighthood; and when he died, in 1591, Sir Edward Osborne was lamented as a good and upright citizen, and one of the worthiest magistrates of the city of London.

His wife brought him a son and two daughters. The latter married into the Offley and Peyton families respectively; while his son, entering the army, and fighting under the banner of the Earl of Essex in quelling a rebellion in Ireland in the year 1599, received from that nobleman the accolade of military knighthood. Sir Hewitt Osborne in his turn married Joyce, daughter of Thomas Fleetwood, Master of the Mint, and sister of Sir William Fleetwood, of Cranford, in Middlesex, who is styled by Collins "Receiver of the Court of Wards." By this lady he had a son, Edward, successively knighted and created a baronet by Charles I., who constituted him Vice-President of the Council for the North of England, and on the breaking out of the Great

Rebellion appointed him Lieutenant-General of the Royal Forces in the North. His son and successor, Sir Thomas, having taken a leading part in bringing about the Restoration, was made by Charles II. Treasurer of the Navy and Lord High Treasurer of the Kingdom, and was also raised to the English and Scottish Peerage as Lord Kiveton, Viscount Dunblane, and Earl of Danby. His lordship took a leading part as chairman of the committee of the House of Peers which, on the abdication of James II., in 1688, declared the throne vacant, and in that capacity warmly advocated the bestowal of the crown on the Prince and Princess of Orange conjointly; he was consequently raised in 1689 to the Marquisate of Carmarthen, and five years later to the Dukedom of Leeds, which thus crowned the fortunes of the lineal descendants and representatives of that Edward Osborne who, just a century before, had left his native town of Ashford to enter as an "apprentice" the household of Sir William Hewitt.

The ducal house of Leeds still continues to thrive and flourish, and its members to this day hold that the adventure of Edward Osborne on London Bridge was the first of a series of successes which retrieved the at one time doubtful prospects of the old Kentish family whom I mentioned at the beginning of this paper. Since that day, as generation after generation has succeeded, the Dukes of Leeds have absorbed into their line the representation, in part or entire, of the noble houses of Conyers, D'Arcy, and Godolphin, to say nothing of more than one descent from the royal house of Plantagenet. But who shall say that the honest and brave apprentice who saved fair Mistress Anne Hewitt from a watery grave is not well worthy to be mentioned in the roll of the house of Osborne, side by side with all and any of them, as one of those ancestors of whom its members have good reason still to be most proud?

AN EPISODE IN THE HISTORY OF THE CATHCARTS.

IF any of my readers will turn to the Cathcart title in the pages of "Burke's Peerage," he will see that the grandfather of the first Earl Cathcart, who was commander-in-chief of the expedition to Copenhagen in 1807, stands recorded as having been Charles, the eighth holder of the ancient Scottish Barony of Cathcart. This barony was conferred in 1447 by James II., of Scotland, on Sir Alan Cathcart, great-great-grandson of another Sir Alan whose valour at the battle of Loudoun Hill, in 1307, is thus immortalised in the ballad:

> "A knight that then was in his route,
> Worthy and widht, stalwart and stout,
> Courteous and fair, and of good fame,
> Sir Alan Cathcart was his name."

Several of this Sir Alan Cathcart's descendants fell on the battle field; for instance, one at Flodden, and another at Pinkie, both of whom were named Alan. In fact the first of the line for four hundred years who was not named Alan by his godfather and godmother at the font, was Charles, the eighth baron, who died in 1740, in the West Indies, whilst acting as commander-in-chief of the British forces. Sir Bernard Burke tells us that this nobleman was twice married; but he is very uncommunicative about his second matrimonial union, saying merely that he "married secondly—no date is given—Mrs Sabine, widow of Joseph Sabine, Esq., of Tring, but by that lady (who married after his decease Lieut. Col. Maguire), he had no issue." In a foot-note he adds "This is the lady of whom the extraordinary story is told of her having been confined for many years by her last husband, Col. Maguire, in a lonely castle in the fastnesses of Ireland." The details of this romantic story I am able to supply, and I trust they will act as a warning to charming widows not to think of marrying more than twice or thrice.

Lady Cathcart's Christian name I am unable to give, but she was one of the four daughters of a certain Mr. Malyn, or Malin, of Southwark, apparently a prosperous tradesman, who had a country villa at Battersea. I have ascertained that she made no less than four adventures on the stormy sea of matrimony, but still she rather outwitted herself in one of her ventures. Her first husband was a certain Mr. James Fleet, of the City of London, who is generally thought to have been the son and heir of Sir John Fleet, the same who filled the civic chair as Lord Mayor in 1693. All that I know about him is that he was lord of the manor of Tewing or Tewin, in Hertfordshire—probably confused by Burke with Tring, in the same county; and that on his death, while still young, she took as her second "lord and master" one of his and her own near neighbours, a Capt. Sabine, younger brother to Gen. Joseph Sabine, of Queenhoo Hall, in Tewin. In 1738 I find her left again a widow, and quite at her own disposal; for she had no children or other incumbrances; and, as both of her husbands had been fairly well off, it is clear that the widow was not a bad speculation, even for

> "A lord, with a coronet of gold
> And garter below the knee."

Accordingly, in 1739, she accepted the proposals of Lord Cathcart, who died, as I have said, before the end of the following year whilst in command of our troops in Dominica. It would have been well indeed for her if on his death she had resolved to give up all further thoughts of conjugal felicity.

But this was not to be. For three long years she wore widow's weeds, and no doubt wore them very becomingly, added to which she was only a little over five and thirty; and, as everybody knows, few women will own to that being "any age at all." But at the end of three years she met with a certain Irish gentleman, who so far captivated her fancy that, although he held, or said he held, a commission in the army of the Queen of Hungary, she bought for him a commission as Lieutenant-Colonel in the British service.

I am able to record her motives for entering into these four successive connections. Her first marriage she contracted in order to please her parents, the second for money, and the third for a coronet and title. As for the fourth marriage, she would often say late in life, when she could afford to jest on such a subject, that she supposed that "the devil owed her a grudge, and wished to punish her for her sins." It may be presumed from what follows that in this supposition she was not very far wrong. It was also said that she managed to rule Lord Cathcart, but that in Colonel Hugh Maguire she at last met with her match, and perhaps something more. The

Hibernian fortune-hunter, like others of our own day, wanted only her money. She had not been married to him many weeks when she found out that he cared not a straw for her, but only for her purse, her jointure, and her diamonds. Apprehending that he had made a plan for carrying her off forcibly, or to put her into a madhouse in order to possess himself of her property, she resolved to be "on the safe side," and accordingly contrived to secret some of her jewels in the tresses of her long dark hair, which she plaited rather carefully. Others she "quilted" in the lining of her petticoats, and constantly wore them on her body, though in daily danger of losing them thereby. The colonel had a clever friend at hand to help him, a *chère amie* of tender years, whom he had trained for his own purposes; and this young lady contrived so far to insinuate herself into the lady's confidence as to discover where her will was kept, and to reveal its whereabouts to the colonel, who of course got a sight of it, and, finding that it was not wholly in his own favour, drew out a pistol and threatened once and again to shoot her.

She now lived in constant fear and dread of her *caro sposo*, though she does not seem to have plucked up enough courage to bolt off from him, and to appeal to her relatives for protection.

In fact, she grew awfully nervous whenever he approached her presence, and life began to be a burden to her.

One day her apprehensions proved not to be altogether groundless, for when the loving pair went out to take their daily airing in the family coach, and she proposed that the coachman should turn the horses' heads homewards, her husband showed his dissent in a rather demonstrative manner, and desired John to drive on further. On and on the coachman drove, and the horses trotted; and in vain she remonstrated that they should never be back at Tewin for dinner, though she had a lady coming to dine. At length the colonel, pulling out a pocket pistol, told her that she might make herself quite easy about dining at home; for "My dear, we are on our way to Chester, and to Chester you shall go with me, whether you like or no." Her expostulations were in vain, and vain too were her efforts, for the servants were in league with their master, who had bribed them with some of her gold.

Day after day passed by, and neither coach nor horses, nor the colonel, nor his lady appeared at Tewin. The neighbours began to suspect that something was wrong, and made inquiry. It was ascertained that on the evening of the day when they were missed, the colonel and his wife were seen twelve or fifteen miles from home, with the horses' heads turned to the north, and the colonel gesticulating as if in a passion with his wife. So they consulted a magistrate in the neighbourhood, who advised that an attorney should be sent after him, armed with one of those legal weapons known as writs of "Habeas corpus," and "Ne exeat regno." The attorney, accompanied by his clerk, was soon upon their track; and as they had travelled with their own horses and by easy stages, he came up with the fugitives before they reached Chester. At a wayside inn, where they were baiting their horses, he presented himself to the landlord, and asked for the room where the runaway couple were lunching. But the colonel was not deficient in expedients. The attorney was admitted by the gentleman, who at first refused to let him see his lady, and threatened him with personal violence. But soon cooling down, on finding that the man of law did not know the lady by sight, he said that if he waited a few minutes he should see her and speak to her, adding "she is going to Ireland with me with her free consent." It did not take many minutes for the colonel to tutor the pretty chambermaid of the inn to personate his wife. On coming into the room, she bowed graciously, and inquired what the lawyer wanted of her. The attorney, as instructed by his employers, asked the supposed captive whether she was going off to Ireland of her own free will? "Perfectly so," said the woman, "what more do you want?" "Nothing, madam," was the answer of the limb of the law, who was glad enough to escape from the room, and beg and obtain her pardon for making such a mistake; and in another half hour he was off on his way back to Hertfordshire, if not having done his business, at all events having earned his pay. So at least he thought.

But the colonel was not so easily satisfied. It struck him that possibly the attorney might recover his senses and find out how he had been deceived, and so turn up again "like a bad penny," and perhaps delay or even stop his progress towards the sister isle; so, in order to make assurance doubly sure, he sent after him two or three stout fellows armed with bludgeons, telling them at the same time to plunder him not only of his purse, but also, above all, of the papers in his pocket. They followed Mr. Attorney, caught him up in a lonely part of the road, and faithfully executed their commission, for they knocked him about severely, and with threats of further injury carried off in triumph the pieces of parchment, which they speedily brought back to the inn.

When the colonel found the two writs actually in his possession, he knew that at length he was safe; and so he pursued his journey, not to Gretna, but to Ireland, the lady not daring to open her lips or show any further sign of an untractable nature.

Poor woman. At Holyhead she was taken on board a fishing smack, and landed after a stormy passage in one of the lesser Irish seaports, where there were no police or Custom House officers to make awkward inquiries or to take notes; and as there were no telegraphs or newspapers, or other means of rapid communication between the two sides of the Channel, the colonel had no difficulty in completing his journey and bringing the lady to the abode which he had destined for her reception. This was a lonely and moated mansion, far away from a town, and well out of the reach of inquisitive and inconvenient neighbours. Indeed it is said that except the butcher's cart, which visited the place about once in ten days, nothing on feet or on wheels ever entered its gates, and that the grass grew thick upon the drive leading up to the front door. Two trusty keepers, a man and his wife, kept watch and ward night and day, upon the unfortunate lady, who was regarded by them as a sort of amiable lunatic, and treated accordingly, though with extreme politeness.

That she was not, however, quite a lunatic Lady Cathcart showed in a very marked way; or, if she was insane, there was "method" and something more "in her madness." Whilst in this state of confinement she was occasionally allowed to walk about the grounds, though the park gates were closed upon her, and she could not scale the park walls. One poor old woman came once a week to dig up the weeds which grew along the garden path; and of her she contrived to make a friend. Through this crone she managed to send the jewels which she had worn in her hair and in the quilting of her petticoats to an acquaintance of former years, by whom they were carefully and honestly preserved.

At last after several years, namely, in 1764, a release came to the unhappy prisoner. The colonel had a fit in the night, and was found at daybreak dead in his bed. That morning saw her a free woman. It was necessary to communicate his death to his kith and kin in order that arrangements might be made for his funeral. They came to the house, and found his widow anxious and ready to quit the spot where she had been so long immured; and they, on their part, were glad to come into a bit of property, even if it were only the lease of a lonely and tumble-down old grange. So she found her way to Dublin, where her jewels were restored to her, and the sale of one of them was sufficient to pay the expense of her journey by ship and the " stage waggon " back to Hertfordshire. She made her way to her former residence at Tewin; but the dinner to which she and her husband were to have sat down on the eventful day of their flight was, of course, no longer on the table; indeed during her forced absence in Ireland the place had been let on lease by the colonel to a " responsible " tenant; and this gentleman declined to turn out until forced to do so by a writ of ejectment, which she brought at the next Hertfordshire assizes. She attended these assizes in person, and the news of the success of her suit was greeted with cheers by large crowds of the good people of Tewin, who insisted on taking the horses out of her carriage and drawing her in triumph through the streets of Hertford.

She lived on for many years at Tewin, where she kept open house for her neighbours, and played a rubber at whist with all and any of them. Late in life she wore a sort of turban, which, though eccentric in its make, suited her features well; and it is among the traditions of the county that when long upwards of eighty, she danced a minuet at the Assembly Rooms at Welwyn with the spirit of a young woman of a quarter of that age. What is better authenticated is that, in 1783, Lady Cathcart gave an annuity of £5 to Tewin School, and that she died in 1789 in the ninety-ninth year of her age. She lies buried in Tewin Church, and the property, which once was her own, now belongs to Lord Cowper.

It will be remembered by readers of Miss Edgworth's novels, that the story of Lady Cathcart's imprisonment is introduced by her under another name, into her humorous Irish tale of "Castle Rackrent." They will not forget how the scapegrace, Sir Kit Rackrent, marries a young English lady for the sake of her fortune, and brings her to Ireland, where he affects to quarrel with her because she professes to dislike sausages, and cannot endure to see pork on the table: the real cause of offence, however, being that she refuses to let him have possession of a diamond trinket, which she keeps about her person. In his well-feigned rage on the score of the sausages, he locks the lady up in her room, and keeps her in close confinement, until one day Sir Kit is brought home dead on a barrow, having been killed in a duel, when the lady regains her liberty.

The story of Lady Cathcart has also been told by Dr. W. Chambers, in a little topographical book, entitled " A Week at Welwyn."

AN EPISODE IN THE NOBLE HOUSE OF HASTINGS.

IN the whole compass of the history of the British aristocracy it would be a difficult task to find a more strange and eccentric personage than the Hon. Henry Hastings—hermit, sportsman, and centenarian in one—the second son of George, fourth Earl of Huntingdon, a cotemporary of Elizabeth, James I., and Charles I. The main facts of his life, and the leading features of his character were for a long time to be found only among the musty manuscripts of Anthony Ashley Cooper, the celebrated Earl of Shaftesbury, in the British Museum. Some of them, however, are pourtrayed in the " Biographia Britannica," and others are to be found in the " Fragment of an Autobiography " by Lord Shaftesbury, published a few years since by Mr.

W. D. Christie; while for the rest, again, we must have recourse to the pages of that scarce and curious book, "The Eccentric."

Mr. Hastings is described by Lord Shaftesbury as being "of Woodlands," a mansion and estate in Dorsetshire, which he appears to have owned. But, instead of residing like a gentleman, on his own property, he preferred, as I have already hinted, the life of a hermit, combining with it that of a sportsman, and accordingly fixed his abode in the New Forest, over which King James gave him a forester's rights, assigning him also a lodge in its green glades to dwell in. In all probability the reason of his strange hermit life was a disappointment in love, which had thrown a dark shadow over his early years. As he died in A.D. 1639, he must have first seen the light of day in 1529, if there be any truth in the assertion that he was a hundred and ten years old at the date of his decease. Of this fact, however, there is no certain proof, for the parish registers in the days of our Stuart sovereigns were kept but carelessly at best; and I have no wish to take up the cudgels and fight over again the vexed question of "centenarianism."

It may be supposed that, singing as he did the good old song, "A life in the woods for me," Henry Hastings kept clear of politics, and blessed his stars that he had not been born an eldest son, and so forced to wear a coronet. His business and tactics lay in quite another direction; and Lord Shaftesbury gives us an amusing peep into the interior of the Hampshire forester's lodge. He says: "His home was of the old fashion, in the midst of a park well-stocked with deer, and near the house rabbits to serve his kitchen; many fish ponds too, and a great store of wood and timber. . . . He kept all manner of sport-hounds that ran buck, fox, hare, otter, and badger; and hawks, long and short-winged; he had also all sorts of nets for fishing; he had a walk in the New Forest, and the manor of Christ Church. This last supplied him with red deer and river fish, but all his neighbours' grounds and royalties were free to him." In fact, he seems pretty well to have realised in his person Pope's idea of the "noble savage" ranging free "in the woods." We are sorry to add, however, that, in spite of his lonely life, he did not bear the very best of characters.

His hall was strewn with marrow-bones, full of hawks' perches, hounds, spaniels, and terriers, and his walls were hung around with the skins of foxes, polecats, rats, and other vermin, which he nailed to the panels. There always stood two large arm-chairs near his fire-place, and it was seldom that they were not occupied with litters of puppies and kittens, which he would on no account allow to be disturbed while in possession. At table he always took a very spare and frugal meal, limiting himself to a single glass of beer or wine. But he never dined unattended by his dogs and cats, to keep which in order he always had laid before his "trencher" a little white stick or wand some fourteen inches long. The windows and corners of his room, Lord Shaftesbury tells us, were filled up with arrows, cross-bows, hunting poles, hawks' hoods and bells, and last (not least) with rows of old green and greasy hats, with their crowns thrust in so as to hold ten or a dozen pheasants' eggs. He made it a point of duty and honour to have at dinner daily all the year round a plate of oysters, which came to him from the neighbouring town of Poole. At the end of the apartment, which served as his parlour and primitive dining hall, there were two doors, the one of which led to his beer and wine closet, and the other into a a room which had been designed as a chapel. But, although a fine Bible, and Foxe's "Book of Martyrs" both lay there in due form, he did not use the place for the purposes of devotion; indeed, if the truth must be told, it was no uncommon thing to find a hen turkey sitting in what ought to have served as a pulpit. When the pulpit was not required for the hen turkey's wants, he would use it as a storehouse for a gammon of bacon, a venison pasty, or a baked apple-pie, of which he was particularly fond.

The rest of the furniture of the house was as old and as strange as its master; and, as he kept no wife or servants, he could " do as he pleased with his own." He liked, however, a friend of his own sphere and rank of life to "drop in" upon him occasionally, especially on a Friday, when " he had the best of sea and fresh water fish," and a " London pudding" by way of cheer. Occasionally, too, he would leave his solitude and go over to Hanley to play bowls with Lord Shaftesbury and other Dorsetshire gentlemen. This, however, did not often happen; for, nearly related though he was to him, Lord Shaftesbury held principles quite opposed to his own, so that they seldom met except to quarrel. In fact, as a writer in the "Eccentric" remarks, "two men could not be more opposite in their dispositions and pursuits; for Henry Hastings, though king-appointed, was an independent character to the backbone, and Lord Shaftesbury used to declare that he never could bear the brutality of his manners, for he was fit only to live by himself as a hopeless misanthrope."

In the inclosure which he fenced off from the surrounding park and forest, though he lived so solitary a life, he contrived to make a bowling-green, where he would play for hours by himself, chalking up the scores of "right against left;" and he must have kept himself *au courant* with the fashions of the day, if it be true that his footpaths were strown with the fragments of old tobacco pipes, since the "noxious weed" was scarcely known in England when he was a boy. To keep up the pleasant delusion that he had company with him, he built in his garden a banqueting room, where, seated by himself, he would give out imaginary toasts, and drink glasses of real wine to imaginary beauties. At times, however, when the fit took him, he would deck up this banqueting room like a booth at a fair, and entertain some of the skilled poachers of the neighbourhood, from whom, though Ranger by the King's appointment, he did not object to receive stray gifts in kind, or hints of a practical nature. And, hermit as he was, he was so far from hating games and diversions, that he would entertain his rough and plebeian guests with cards and dice, giving each of them one glass of "mum" or beer, and no more.

In the evening, by way of supper, we are told that he would take a single glass of sack, seasoned with the syrup of gillyflowers, which he stirred with a sprig of rosemary. The troubles of the times never touched or disturbed him; safe in the glades of his Hampshire forest, he had forgotten the King, and the Court had forgotten him. A short time before his death he rode on horseback, and went a day's journey in order to hear an old huntsman, who was himself turned ninety, relate the death of a stag that was said to be older than either of the pair. If so, the united ages of huntsman, stag, and Hastings must have been as near as possible three hundred years. There is a portrait of this Henry Hastings at St. Giles's House, near Wimborne, Dorsetshire, the seat of Lord Shaftesbury, and an engraving from the portrait will be found in the second volume of Hutchins' "History of Dorset." Tradition still records the fact, that, in spite of his lonely life and patched dress, he showed in his manners the breeding of a regular gentleman, except in the one matter of swearing. Altogether Henry Hastings must be pronounced to have been an original, such a man as you would not be likely to meet twice in a lifetime. Lord Shaftesbury describes him as having been "low of stature, very strong and very active, with reddish flaxen hair." He tells us that "his clothes were always made of green cloth," possibly in allusion to the fabled connection of his ancestor with Robin Hood and Little John, with Sherwood Forest and suits of "Lincoln green;" and he adds with a spice of sly satire, which he seems thoroughly to enjoy, that "all of the latter, even when new, were never worth five pounds."

Had Mr. Hastings married and had sons, it is more than probable that the present century would never have heard of the celebrated peerage case which gave the earldom of Huntingdon to the grandfather of the present head of the house.

THOMAS PITT, LORD CAMELFORD.

THE sad story of the wasted life and tragical end of Thomas, second Lord Camelford, is one which cannot fail to awaken interest in readers of every rank, as an instance of a man who, though largely gifted with good natural qualities, and placed in a situation of life where, with good sense and right principles to guide him, he might have attained a high position in the State, chose to sacrifice all his prospects to the waywardness of his disposition, and fell a martyr to his own folly.

Lord Camelford was the great-grandson of Robert Pitt, the famous governor of Madras, who acquired a large fortune in India the best part of two centuries ago by the advantageous purchase of a certain diamond, which he brought back with him to England, and eventually sold at a great profit to the Duke of Orleans, at that time Regent of France. His lordship not only held a seat in the House of Peers, but he was extensively connected with some of the first families in the kingdom. His grandfather's brother was the "great commoner," William Pitt, and afterwards first Earl of Chatham. His father was consequently first cousin to William Pitt the younger and to the second Earl of Chatham; and his own sister, Anne Pitt, was the wife of Lord Grenville, who, a few years after the date of which I write, became first Lord of the Treasury and head of the Ministry of "all the talents." The father, Thomas Pitt, the first Lord Camelford (so created in 1784) owned the fine family estate of Boconnoc, in Cornwall, which devolved upon his son, together with the coronet, while he was still in his minority.

Born in 1775, he received the first rudiments of his education under a tutor in the Canton of Berne, in Switzerland, where even as a child he showed a spirit and temper which, though manly and vigorous, was peculiarly moody, wayward, and untractable. He did not bear the character of a manageable boy at the Charterhouse, (then under Dr. Berdmore), to which he was removed when about ten or twelve years old, and where he did not stay long, having shown an early taste for the roving and adventurous life of a sailor. It was not a difficult matter for a cousin of the premier to obtain a commission in the Royal Navy, and accordingly in 1789 we find him joining, as a midshipman, the frigate "Guardian" commanded by the gallant Capt. Riou, and laden with stores for the then infant colony of convicts which was settled at Botany Bay. The calamity which befell that ship was well calculated to inure the young seaman to the perils of the sea; and even at that time he showed the same contempt for danger which marked his career throughout, and which often partook rather of the nature of recklessness than of bravery. I need only say here that when all endeavours to save the "Guardian" seemed hopeless, and her commander gave leave to such of her crew as chose to take to the boats, young Pitt was one of those who to the number of ninety resolved to stand by the ship and to share her fate with her gallant commander. In the end, after an escape little short of miraculous, the ship made the Cape of Good Hope, in the condition of a wreck, and in September, 1790, the survivors found their way to England.

Undaunted by the dangers which he had encountered in the "Guardian," young Pitt on reaching London went straight to the Admiralty, and bringing such family influence as he could to bear upon "My Lords," obtained an appointment to join an exploring voyage which was fitting out under Capt. Vancouver. He accompanied that officer in the ship "Discovery" during part of his distant voyage; but through his refractoriness and disobedience of orders, the result of his wayward and obstinate temper, he provoked his commanding officer to treat him with a severity which he would not endure.

Accordingly, quitting the "Discovery" in the Indian seas, he joined the "Resistance," commanded by Sir E. Pakenham, and soon gained the rank of lieutenant. It was while serving on board this ship that he heard the news of his father's death, and of his accession to the honours of the peerage. On returning home in 1796, the first thing he did was to send a challenge to his late commanding officer, Captain Vancouver, which that gentleman, on professional grounds, was obliged to decline. The wound, however, rankled deep in the breast of Lord Camelford, who threatened to chastise his superior officer. Doubtless, had he been a plain, untitled lieutenant—Brown, Jones, or Robinson—he would have been cashiered for disrespect; but then he was a Pitt, and cousin to the First Lord of the Treasury, so what could poor Captain Vancouver do? He did the only thing possible, namely, to sit down and digest his wrath; and the end was that he died of grief and pain, instead of a pistol-shot.

Having attained the rank of commander, when he had yet to learn how to command himself, though he had reached the "age of discretion," Lord Camelford was appointed next to the sloop "Favourite," on the West Indian station. We next hear of him at Antigua, where, on Jan. 13, 1798, the "Favourite" and the "Perdrix" (Captain Fahie) were lying at anchor in harbour. Captain Fahie, it so happened, was absent at St. Kitts, and had left his lieutenant, Mr. Peterson, in charge of the "Perdrix." Lord Camelford, whether in the discharge of his duty or in mere wantonness, as being the senior officer, and consequently in command, issued some trifling order which the lieutenant did not feel bound to obey. Lord Camelford must have been a summary disciplinarian, for he called out his marines, and, asking Peterson if he meant to obey his order, and obtaining no answer or a refusal, he shot him dead on the spot. Lieutenant Peterson was much beloved in Antigua; and the excited populace were hardly restrained from dealing summary and probably fatal chastisement on his lordship; but they were calmed by an assurance that an inquiry into the matter should be made by court-martial. But the coroner's jury having brought in a verdict to the effect that Peterson had "lost his life in a mutiny," and the court-martial having "honourably" acquitted his lordship, the Admiralty at home let the affair pass into oblivion. Again it was not a Brown, Jones, or Robinson, but a Pitt who had shot the lieutenant; and the Pitts were a "heaven-born" race. Some say, I know, that "sin is not sin in a duchess," and possibly the saying may be true; probably it is equally true that "killing is (or was) no murder" when wrought by the hand of a peer of the realm. I doubt if the same law would hold good now, as that which appears to have prevailed some four score years back in the history of the British navy.

After his acquittal, Lord Camelford resumed for a time the command of his ship, but soon threw it up, at the same time quitting the profession in which he had earned such a character for daring and for discipline. "While in the service," says a writer of the time," his personal appearance was distinguished by the same eccentricity which marked his conduct through life. His dress consisted of a lieutenant's plain coat, without shoulder knots, and its buttons were as green with verdigris as the ship's bottom itself. His head was shaved close, and he wore an enormous gold-laced cocked hat." It deserves to be remembered to his credit, that, though he was so severe a disciplinarian, he showed himself particularly attentive to the comfort and relief of the sick.

He had not long returned to London when he took it into his head to plan a mad freak, which if he had been allowed to put it into execution, would probably have cost him his life, and have added seriously to the complications of the war with France, which just then was at its fiercest. His plan was to repair to Paris, and there, in the midst of that city, to attack personally and kill the rulers of the Republic. With this object in view, he took coach to Dover, where he arranged with a boatman to convey him across the Channel for twelve guineas, though the law at that time was so stringent as to make the very act of embarkation for France a capital offence. The compact, however, was betrayed to a local collector of the revenue, who accompanied his lordship to the boat, and arrested him in the act of stepping into it. The triumphant " collector" lost no time in carrying his lordship back to London in a post-chaise, under a strong guard, and conveying him to the office of the Duke of Portland, at Whitehall. A meeting of the Privy Council was summoned, and I read in the account which I have already quoted, that "after several examinations his lordship was discharged from custody, the Lords of the Council being satisfied that, however irregular his conduct, his intentions were only such as he had represented them to be, and that he had no other object in view except that of rendering a service to the country. His Majesty's pardon, therefore, was issued under the Great Seal of the Kingdom, discharging his lordship from all the penalties which he had incurred under an Act recently passed, which, without reference to motive, made the mere act of embarking for France a capital crime."

This was in January, 1799; and at least two months appear to have elapsed before Lord Camelford's name was again brought in any marked manner before the public, though he continued to live on in London, indulging by day and night too in a series of practical and sometimes offensive jokes, such as those for which the late Lord Waterford in our own day made himself so notorious. At one time I find him causing a riot at the box office of Drury Lane (April 2, 1799), and insulting and assaulting one of the audience—a freak for which his lordship was tried before Lord Kenyon and a special jury, and sentenced to pay a fine of £500, though he had for his counsel that consummate advocate, Mr. Thomas Erskine, afterwards Lord Chancellor Erskine. On another occasion, when he and his boon companion, Captain Barrie, were returning home late at night, or rather early in the morning, as they passed through Cavendish Square, they found the "Charleys" asleep. Of course it did not take a minute to wake them up—which was all very right—and to thrash them—which was all very wrong. At last the "Charleys" sprang their rattles, and other more vigilant guardians of the West End streets rushed up; but it was not till they were overpowered by ten to two that Lord Camelford and his comrade were led off to the station-house. Next morning, as a matter of course, they were brought up to the Marlborough Street office, where a present of a guinea a-piece to the injured "Charleys" enabled the sitting magistrate to declare the offenders discharged, with a warning not to repeat such conduct.

There was nothing in which Lord Camelford took greater delight than in standing out in direct contrast to the general public, and finding himself in a minority of one. Had he frequented the House of Lords, he would, no doubt, have often been able to gratify this whim; but his tastes led him to associate not with his "peers," in either sense of the term, but with the "ignobile vulgus" of the London streets. For instance, though he had wished to go to Paris in order to end the war by a single blow, yet in 1801, when all London was lit up by a general illumination, no persuasion of his friends or of his landlord could induce Lord Camelford to suffer lights to be placed in the windows of his rooms. He lodged over a grocer's shop in New Bond Street; and in vain did the grocer and his wife protest; he remained firm to his silly and wayward resolve. The mob, of course, attacked the house and saluted his windows with showers of stones. Irritated at the assault, Lord Camelford rushed out among the crowd with a pistol in his hand, and it seemed as if the festive day was doomed to be marked with blood. At last, however, his friend Barrie induced him to exchange the pistol for a stout cudgel, with which he laid about him right and left, until at length, overpowered by numbers, he was rolled over and over in the gutter, and was glad at last to beat a retreat indoors, filthy and crest-fallen.

In general, Lord Camelford was not one of that amiable class of young men who return to their nests at the end of the business of the day and "dine at home" quietly and respectably. On the contrary, he lived chiefly at clubs and coffee houses, where his presence had at least one advantage, namely, that of holding in check the insolence of the young puppies who haunted such *rendezvous* and gave themselves airs and graces. Indeed, whoever was brought into contact with his lordship in those days when pistols were often carried, and duelling was in vogue, was speedily made to feel that he had better be careful as to what passed his lips, lest in an unguarded moment he should have to expiate with his blood the slightest slip of the tongue.

His irritable disposition and obstinate temper not only led him to quarrels and encounters beyond all number, but in the end paved the way for the final catastrophe of his tragical death. It appears that for some time Lord Camelford had been acquainted with a certain lady named Simmons. Some officious person, either from a silly habit of talking, or out of sheer malice, represented to the touchy nobleman that a friend of his named Best had said to the lady something to his disadvantage. This ill-timed piece of information nettled his lordship, and rankled in his breast so much that on the 6th of March, 1804, on meeting Mr. Best at the Prince of Wales's Coffee-house, he went up to him and said aloud, and in a tone to be heard by the bystanders, "I find, Sir, that you have been speaking of me in the most unwarrantable terms." Mr. Best simply replied that he was quite unconscious of having done anything to deserve such a charge. Lord Camelford declared that he well knew what he had said to Mrs. Simmons, and called him a " liar, a scoundrel, and ruffian."

The use of epithets such as these, according to the established code of laws then current in society, left but one course open to Mr. Best, and a hostile meeting was at once arranged for the following morning. Each of the parties having appointed his " second," it was left, as usual, to the latter to fix the time and place. These were seven o'clock in the morning, and the fields behind Holland House at Kensington.

Meantime every means was being put in motion to supersede the necessity of a duel, or to prevent its occurrence, or at all events to stop it before a fatal result should ensue; and I regret to add that it seems to have been wholly Lord Camelford's fault that these efforts proved unavailing. Later in the evening, Mr. Best, though he had been so grossly and wantonly insulted, sent to his lordship a strong assurance that the information which he had received was quite groundless, and that, as he had acted under a false impression, he should be quite satisfied if his lordship would withdraw the strong epithets which he had applied to him. But Lord Camelford refused to accept this kindly and sensible offer. Mr. Best then left the coffee house, and some mutual friends or witnesses among the bystanders lodged an information at Marlborough Street.

Notwithstanding the magistrates were thus early let into the secret, it appears that no steps were taken to prevent the hostile encounter until nearly two o'clock in the morning, by which time his lordship, who had gained a fair stock of experience in "matters of honour" by this time, had of course taken good care to be "off," having ordered a bed at a tavern near Oxford Street.

During the night he made his will, bequeathing his estates to his sister, Lady Grenville. In this he inserted a clause in which, to do him justice, he wholly acquits his antagonist of blame in the affair, expressly declares that the quarrel was of his own seeking, and desires that in the event of his own death, and the law being put into force against Mr. Best, the King may be petitioned and requested in his (Lord C.'s) name to extend to him the royal pardon.

Early on the following morning, at the coffee-house in Oxford Street, Mr. Best made another effort to prevail on his lordship to retract the expressions which he had used. "Camelford," said he, "we have been friends, and I know the generosity and the unsuspiciousness of your nature. Upon my honour you have been imposed upon by Mrs. Simmons; do not insist on using expressions which in the end must cause the death of either you or me." To this Lord Camelford merely replied dryly, " Best, all this is mere child's play; the matter must go on."

Unable to come to terms at the coffee house in Oxford Street, the two principals mounted their horses, and rode along the Uxbridge Road, past the wall which then bounded Kensington Gardens, as far as the " Horse and Groom," a little beyond Notting Hill turnpike-gate. At the "Horse and Groom" they dismount, cross the road, and proceed at a quick pace along the path leading to the fields behind Holland House. The seconds measure the ground, and Lord Camelford and Mr. Best take up their positions at thirty paces. The sun has lately risen, and one or two of the outdoor servants of Holland House are about the grounds; but while they wonder and stare the signal is given, and Lord Camelford fires. Either designedly or not, he fires without effect, and Mr. Best is a living man. A quarter of a minute elapses, the signal is repeated, and Lord Camelford falls forward on the ground. He is not dead, but he is mortally wounded: and oh, irony of ironies! he declares that he " is satisfied." He shakes hands with his antagonist, who runs to pick him up: "Best, I am a dead man, and you have killed me; but I freely forgive you—the fault was mine."

It was now time for Mr. Best to beat a retreat, and one of Lord Holland's gardeners was despatched for a surgeon. A chair was soon procured; and seated in it, and supported by the bystanders, Lord Camelford was carried off to Little Holland House, the residence of Mr. Otty, where he was attended by two surgeons, Mr. Thompson and Mr. Knight, of Kensington. In an hour more his faithful friend Captain Barrie was beside his bed, and so was his cousin, the Rev. Mr. Cockburn.

From the first the surgeons gave little or no hope that the wound would prove anything other than mortal. The ball could not be extracted, and he lingered in great agony for nearly three days, when death put an end to his sufferings. So died Thomas Lord Camelford, at the early age of twenty-nine, by a death which, though not actually self-inflicted, was brought on by his own wayward obstinacy.

The estimate formed by Mr. Cockburn as to Lord Camelford's real character, and his testimony to the sincerity of the penitence of his deathbed, are alike striking. He writes:—

"Lord Camelford was a man whose real character was but little known to the world; his imperfections and his follies were often brought before the public, but the counterbalancing virtues he manifested were but little heard of. Though violent to those whom he imagined to have wronged him, yet to his acquaintances he was mild, affable, and courteous: a stern adversary, but the kindest and most generous of friends. Slow and cautious in determining upon any important step while deliberating, he was most attentive to the advice of others, and easily brought over to their opinion; when, however, his resolutions were once taken, it was almost impossible to turn him from his purpose. That warmth of disposition which prompted him so unhappily to great improprieties, prompted him also to the most lively efforts of active benevolence. From the many prisons in the metropolis, from the various receptacles of human misery, he received numberless petitions, and no petition ever came in vain. He was often the dupe of the designing and crafty supplicant, but he was more often the reliever of real sorrow, and the soother of unmerited woe. Constantly would he make use of that influence which rank and fortune gave him with the Government, to interfere in the behalf of those malefactors whose crimes had subjected them to punishment, but in whose cases appeared circumstances of alleviation. He was passionately fond of science, and though his mind while a young seaman had been little cultivated, yet in later years he had acquired a prodigious fund of information upon almost every subject connected with literature. In early life he had gloried much in puzzling the chaplains of ships in which he served, and to enable him to gain such triumphs he had read all the sceptical books he could procure; and thus his mind became involuntarily tainted with infidelity. As his judgment grew more matured, he discovered of himself the fallacy of his own reasonings, he became convinced of the importance of religion, and Christianity was the constant subject of his reflections, his reading and conversation.... I wish with all my soul that the unthinking votaries of dissipation and infidelity could have been present at the deathbed of this poor man; could have heard his expressions of contrition after misconduct, and of his reliance on the mercy of his Creator: could have heard his dying exhortation to one of his intimate friends to live in future a life of peace and virtue: I think it would have made impressions on their minds, as it did on mine, not easily to be effaced."

On the day after his death an inquest was held

on the body of his lordship, when, strange as it may sound to the ears of those who have read this brief story, twelve wise and enlightened inhabitants of the country village of Kensington, for such it then was, brought in a verdict of "wilful murder against some person or persons unknown."

It is evident that Lord Camelford had in him the elements of a good naval officer, if his proud, obstinate, and wayward spirit could only have bent itself to the rules and requirements of the service. But from a child he would never obey, or fall in with even the reasonable wishes of parents and tutors. At school the same headstrong and wilful nature cropped out which he exhibited in the navy; and he was true to it to the very end. In the codicil to his will, which he dictated whilst writhing in his mortal agony, he declared that, while other individuals desired to be buried in their native land, he wished to be interred "in a country far distant—in a spot not near to the haunts of men, but where the surrounding scenery might smile upon his remains."

But in this matter he was not destined to have his own way. Lord Camelford's body was brought back from Kensington to Camelford House, at the top of Park Lane, nominally his town residence, though he preferred his bachelor quarters in Bond Street; and thence it was taken and deposited in the vaults of St. Anne's, Soho. Owing to the war, effect could not be given to his desire for interment in the soil of Switzerland, and his body still lies where it was first interred, in a magnificent coffin, covered with gorgeous red velvet, and surmounted by a coronet. It is perhaps the more necessary for me to record this fact, as the contrary has been asserted by Mr. Charles Reade, in an article on Lord Camelford in "Belgravia" for May, 1876, who says that the body was wrapped up in a common fish-basket, and that it is not known now what became of it. But the mystery is no mystery at all; for I saw the coffin, or at all events what the verger told me was the coffin of Lord Camelford, in the vaults under St. Anne's, Soho, about the year 1860; and the coffin might or might not have contained a fish-basket in the place of a "shell." I may add that a letter from the courteous owner of his Lordship's seat in Cornwall, the Hon. George M. Fortescue, assures me that he never heard of any attempt, or even desire, on the part of the relations of the eccentric nobleman, to bring his remains again into the light of day.

His fine property of Boconnoc Park near Lostwithiel, in Cornwall he left to his sister Anne, the wife of Lord Grenville. She outlived him sixty years, dying in the full possession of her faculties, at the age of ninety, in the year 1863. At her death, she bequeathed the estate to her husband's nephew, Mr. Fortescue, the gentleman mentioned above.

AN EPISODE IN THE EARLDOM OF PEMBROKE.

NEXT to the Howards, who undoubtedly stand first and foremost in the roll of English nobility, with their forty coronets all fairly won by them in four hundred years, no family rises higher in respect of its honours than that of the Herberts. For not only do its male descendants in our day wear the coronets of three earldoms— those of Pembroke, Montgomery, and Carnarvon —but within a period quite historic they have borne at least two more, namely, those of Powis and Torrington, both now extinct in the male line; to say nothing of other dignities in the lower grade of barons, as Lords Herbert of Cherbury, Lords Herbert of Cardiff, Lords Herbert of Shurland, and, by recent creation, Lords Herbert of Lea. In addition to this they have made alliances with nearly all the greatest and noblest of our titled houses—the Talbots, the Greys, Dukes of Suffolk, the Sidneys, the Villierses, the Howards, the Arundells, the Paulets, the Scropes, and the Spencers; so that the present Lord Pembroke, although not undisputed head and representative of the house of Herbert, has come, through the intermarriages of his ancestors, to hold four ancient baronies in fee, as Lord Ross of Kendal, Parr, Marmion, and St. Quentin. How all this comes about it would not be easy to show in detail without drawing out for my readers a long genealogical tree; and those who wish to examine my statement for themselves can verify my words by the authority of Sir Bernard Burke, whose assertion of the fact, I own, is sufficient for myself.

If they will turn to his "Peerage" and his "Landed Gentry," they will find that; in addition to the honours above mentioned, the main stem of the Herberts has produced several untitled branches of high worth and renown, such, for instance, as the Herberts of St. Julian's and of Magor, in Monmouthshire, the Herberts of Llanarth, in Wales, and of Cahirnane, in Ireland. Above all, with respect to the Herberts of Muckross, near Killarney, my friend "Ulster" writes as follows: "Since the merging of the elder branch of the Herberts in the family of Clive, by the marriage of the heiress of the last Herbert, Earl of Powis, with the son of the celebrated general, Lord Clive, the chieftainship of the name seems undoubtedly to rest with the Herberts of Muckross, in the county of Kerry, who are descended from Thomas Herbert of Kilcuagh, who went to Ireland under the care and patronage of his relative, Lord Herbert of Cherbury." And then he proceeds to trace the descent of this Thomas Herbert from the eldest son of Sir Richard Herbert of Colebroke, only brother of William, Earl of Pembroke of the first creation, who—as may be read in the pages of Speed and Holinshed—suffered largely in purse and pocket for his adherence to the House of York in the Wars of the Roses.

It should be added that, while one of the earl's coronets belonging to the Herberts—namely, that of Powis—for a short time blossomed into that of a marquis, one of the fair Countesses of Pembroke was even more highly honoured by the muses; for to her Sir Philip Sidney dedicated his "Arcadia," while Ben Jonson immortalized her memory in the well-known verses that will live as long as the English tongue:

> "Underneath this marble herse
> Lies the subject of all verse:
> Sidney's sister, Pembroke's mother.
> Death, ere thou hast slain another
> Wise and fair and good as she,
> Time shall throw a dart at thee."

Further, it should be recorded that no less than two brothers, successively Earls of Pembroke, were also in succession the "honoured lords and chancellors" of the University of Oxford, where a noble statue of one of them still graces the gallery of the Bodleian Library; and the reader will need scarcely to be reminded that the father of the present Earl of Pembroke was the good, the kind, the courteous, and amiable Sidney Herbert, the rising statesman and future premier of England, to whom it was no honour to be created Lord Herbert of Lea, so high did he stand before with Englishmen of all shades of politics.

When a single house can show so many of its members ennobled both by titles and by the higher dignity of personal merit, it is scarcely worth while to record such facts as that one Lord Pembroke was Lord Chamberlain to the Household to Charles I., and that another was "chosen to carry the sword called 'curtana' at the coronation of George I." However, some of my fair readers may possibly like to "make a note" of them. Let me, however, remind them one and all that the surname of the house ennobled by so many creations, and spread through so many branches, is said to be derived from two Anglo-Saxon words, "Her" and "Bert" meaning "illustrious lord," a derivation in their case not wholly false in fact. I suppose too that, in order to do justice to antiquity and to show my respect for "blue blood," I ought to add that, according to the heralds, the Herberts are sprung from one Herbert, Count of Vermandois, who came over to England with the Conqueror, and held the office of Chamberlain to William Rufus. He is mentioned in the roll of Battle Abbey, as rewarded with a large grant of land in Hampshire, and as having married a daughter of Stephen, Count of Blois, granddaughter of William I. The first of the Herberts born in England, it appears, was his son, Herbert Fitz-Herbert, called Herbert of Winchester, who became Treasurer and Chamberlain to Henry I. His son held the same office under the second Henry, and his great grandson was summoned to Parliament as a Baron in A.D. 1294. If this be so, in all probability either Mr. Herbert of Muckross, or Lord Pembroke himself, might rightly put in a claim for a barony in fee nearly as old as that of De Ros.

I must, however, pass by all notice of him, and of his descendant, William Herbert, first Earl of Pembroke, Chief Forester of Snowdon, and Constable of Conway Castle, the staunch adherent of the house of York, who, falling into the hands of the Lancastrians after the battle of Dane's Moor, in 1469, suffered attainder, and was beheaded at Banbury. His grandson, William, was installed a Knight of the Garter, and created Lord Herbert of Cardiff, and eventually obtained in his favour a fresh creation of the Earldom of Pembroke. He married a sister of Catharine Parr (the last wife of Henry VIII.), and became one of the most powerful noblemen of his day, taking an active part in public affairs as a soldier and as a statesman. It is recorded of him that " he rode on the 17th of February, 1552-3, to his mansion of Baynard Castle, in London, with a retinue of three hundred horsemen, of which one hundred were gentlemen in plain blue cloth, with chains of gold, and badges of a dragon on their sleeves." Dying in 1570, he was buried in Old St. Paul's Cathedral, and with such magnificence that, if we may trust the old chronicler Stow, the mourning given at his funeral cost the large sum, at that time, of £2000. It was this nobleman's son Henry, the second earl of the new creation, and also a

Knight of the Garter, whose third wife was the lady mentioned above as

"Sidney's sister, Pembroke's mother."

But from all these brilliant and pleasant reminiscences I must pass to my promised "episode" in the noble house of Pembroke. It is by no means a pleasant one to relate, or, I fear, a creditable one to the otherwise spotless shield of the noble Herberts—men almost without exception *sans peur et sans reproche*.

It appears that Philip, the seventh wearer of the coronet of Pembroke, who came to the title in the reign of Charles II., stood out with an evil prominence even among the riotous and debauched nobles who hung about the Whitehall and St. James's of that day. In our own time we have seen a Lord Kingston month after month quarrelling at Charing-cross with Hansom-cab drivers, and a Lord Waldegrave and a Lord Waterford getting up rows in the Haymarket, knocking down policemen, and using their fists pretty freely in street brawls at the West-end— not always quite defensively. But these were comparatively innocents—quite "lambs," as they would be called at Nottingham—by the side of Philip, seventh Earl of Pembroke and fourth Earl of Montgomery. Of him we learn a little in a certain book of "State Trials" which gives us a peep at his character. Let me only preface my "episode" with one remark, that he was the grandson, not of the great Lord Pembroke, the ornament of the Court of King James I., but of his younger brother, who "began life as one of James's favourites and parasites, was ennobled by the title of Earl of Montgomery, and finished a career in all its parts alike contemptible by being the first member of the peerage after the fall of the monarchy who sought (and obtained) a seat in the House of Commons."

Philip, this nobleman's grandson, who became Earl of Pembroke as well as of Montgomery, on the death of his half-brother in 1674, according to an entry in the Lord's Journals, Jan. 28, 1678, was committed to the Tower "for uttering such horrid and blasphemous words, and for such other actions proved upon oath, as are not fit to be repeated in any Christian assembly." Bishop Kennet explains at length what these blasphemies were,* and I will not trouble my readers by

* It is right to add that in consequence of this affair, "to show their lordships' great sense and abhorrency against blasphemy," it was ordered that a bill be brought into the House "for the severe punishment of all blasphemers for the time to come." Such a bill was brought in, but from some cause or other was allowed to drop. It is almost too good to hope that even in this embryo state it had gained its end.

retailing them; I will only say that in a petition dated from the Tower, which is to be found no doubt in the Journals of the House of Peers, Lord Pembroke "humbly implored pardon of God, the King, and of this House," and accordingly, after a month spent in durance vile, was released, and "had leave to come to his place in Parliament."

It is remarkable that, among the grounds on which the noble Earl begged for his release, he pleaded the fact that "his health was much impaired by long restraint." Let us see what follows. Such an invalid is he that he has been out of prison only a few days when a complaint is made to the House of Lords by a Mr. Philip Rycaut to the effect that, "he being to visit a friend in the Strand, whilst he was at the door taking his leave, the Earl of Pembroke came up to the door and with his fist, without any provocation, struck the said Philip Rycaut such a blow upon the eye as almost knocked it out, and afterwards knocked him down, and then fell upon him with such violence that he almost stifled him with his grips in the dirt; that his lordship then likewise drew his sword and was in danger of killing him, had he not slipped into the house and the door been shut upon him." The wounded man brings his petition to a close by humbly begging the House " to be an asylum to him" and give him leave to proceed against the Earl according to law. In the end his lordship was bound over in £2000 to keep the peace towards Mr. Rycaut and the rest of His Majesty's subjects for twelve months.

But unhappily, almost before Mr. Rycaut had been able to invoke the aid of the House of Peers, Lord Pembroke had got into another and far more serious scrape; for the House of Lords on 1st of March following received a petition from Lord Pembroke himself, complaining that at a coroner's inquest held on the body of Nathaniel Cony, gentleman, he had been charged with causing that person's death, evidently implying that he had received an affront which he ought not to brook as a peer.

Next day a committee of the "Law Lords" was appointed to consider the question thus raised; but so far were they from taking his lordship's view, that on the 6th it was resolved " that a commission of oyer and terminer should be issued under the Great Seal for the indictment of Philip, Earl of Pembroke, for killing and slaying Nathaniel Cony." On the 19th the Lord Chancellor informed the House that the Grand jury had found him guily of " felony and murder," and a Lord High Steward—Lord Finch, afterwards Earl of Nottingham—having been appointed in due form for the purpose, Lord Pembroke was put upon his trial, just as within the memory of most of us the late Lord Cardigan was tried for the murder of Captain Tuckett.

It is needless here to recount the legal details of the affair; they may be found at full length by those who are curious in such things in the book of "State Trials." It is enough to say that the indictment charged the noble earl with "feloniously, wilfully, and of malice beforethought, striking, bruising, and kicking, killing and murdering the said Nathaniel Cony, in the parish of St. Martin's-in-the-Fields, against the peace of our sovereign lord the King, his crown and dignity." It appears that without any provocation, while drinking in Long's Tavern in the Haymarket, Lord Pembroke first insulted and then assaulted Mr. Cony, next knocked him down, and ended by kicking him when prostrate. The poor man died a few days after, in spite of all that the doctors and "chirurgeons" could do. The trial, happily, was not dragged out to such a length as that of a certain "claimant" of the present day at Westminster; the case against Lord Pembroke having been opened by Sir Wm. Dolben, Recorder of London, in his capacity of King's Serjeant-at-Law, the prosecution was conducted by the Attorney-General Sir William Jones, and the witnesses having been examined, and the evidence against him having been summed up by Sir Francis Winnington, in a day or two the turbulent and quarrelsome nobleman who had thus tarnished the shield of the Herberts was found guilty of manslaughter; forty of their lordships finding that verdict, while six were for finding him guilty of the higher offence, and eighteen pronounced him "not guilty."

It so happened that, although if he had been found guilty of murder that plea would not have saved him (as witness the cases of Lord Stourton and Lord Ferrers), yet as the law then stood it was competent for a member of the Upper House to plead in arrest of judgment for manslaughter " the privilege of his peerage;" so he got off scot free, and the Lord High Steward put an end to the farce of the trial by breaking his staff according to ancient custom.

But the danger that he had run on this occasion did not cure Lord Pembroke of his fondness for tavern brawls. In the following November a quarrel over their cups arose between his lordship and the Earl of Dorset; and, as usual, the quarrel seemed likely to end in a duel. The matter being happily brought under the notice of the House of Peers, before any blood had been spilt, their lordships resolved that both of the belligerent parties should be "confined to their respective houses or lodgings till further orders;" and finally, on a full consideration of the whole affair, it was ordered that the confinement of the Earl of Dorset and that of the Earl of Pembroke should be "taken off," and that the latter should have leave given him "to retire himself to his house at Wilton." This was not, one would think, a very severe punishment for such a miscreant; and many a man in the humbler ranks of middle life in our own day would be glad to be let off for two serious and one fatal assault by honorary banishment to some pleasant grounds and a park, in Wiltshire or elsewhere. Such an ostracism indeed would be a thing to be envied by most of us, if unaccompanied by a *tâche* or a stain, but scarcely otherwise.

Whether the noble Earl took advantage of the kind permission thus given to him to "retire himself" from the temptations of "high life in London," does not appear. It may, however, be presumed that he took the hint, as we do not hear of him playing such mad pranks again in the parish of St. Martin's-in-the-Fields. He died in 1683, when his titles, honours, and estates passed to a younger and far worthier brother,

Thomas, who became the eighth Earl. He restored the ancient reputation of the family; for, besides holding several high offices in the State, including that of Lord High Admiral and the Lord Lieutenancy of Ireland, his distinction in the world of literature and science procured for him the chair of the Royal Society. His name too is worthy of remembrance, as the collector of that magnificent gallery of sculptures and other antiquities which has for two centuries given an envied celebrity to the fine old seat of Wilton House, the home and haunt of the English muses, and renowned alike for its pictures and art treasures, and as the spot where Sidney wrote the greater part of his " Arcadia." The titles of Pembroke and Montgomery have since descended in his line, and it may well be hoped that the youthful Earl of Pembroke will do no discredit hereafter to the honoured name of his own lamented father, Sidney Herbert.

And what about the issue of Philip, the seventh Earl? Happily, he left no male descendants to carry on the polluted stream, which for centuries had flowed so purely in the veins of the Herberts. He married one of the loose and frail beauties of the Court of Charles the Second, Henriette de Querouaille, a sister of the notorious Duchess of Portsmouth. This lady, who survived her husband nearly half a century, left a daughter, who married the second Lord Jeffries, son of the infamous Judge Jeffries, by whom she became the mother of Henriette Louisa, Countess of Pomfret, a title now extinct.

THE RISE OF THE ROTHSCHILDS.

AS more than one fair lady of the House of Rothschild has lately married into what I suppose may be styled our Christian aristocracy, a short account of the steps of the ladder by which the Rothschilds in less than a century have climbed from poverty to the highest pinnacle of commercial success may not be without interest at the present moment. The main facts are not new to the world, but the details I have reason to believe will be found new by very many, if not most of my readers; and I will therefore proceed with my story, with only a word of preface—namely, that for most of them I am indebted to my worthy friend Mr. Frederick Martin, the author of the "Statesman's Year Book," and of other useful works too numerous to mention.

In the centre of the ancient city of Frankfort-on-the-Maine is a narrow lane not unlike Holywell Street, in the Strand, or Maryleport Street, Bristol, but which, a hundred years ago, was not only one of the narrowest, but one of the dirtiest and filthiest in Europe. It was called the "Judengasse," or Jews' lane—the name denoting the fact that the Jewish population were forced to live in one part of the town, analogous to the "Ghetto" at Rome, and to the "Jewry" of the city of London in the middle ages. In that street, in the year 1743, was born Meyer Amschel Rothschild, the founder of that great house which holds in its hands the destinies of European nations more truly than the ephemeral emperors and kings of our day. An empire may fall at Sedan; a king may abdicate at Madrid; and the imperial and regal glories pass away as a dream; but Juvenal long ago crowned money as a Queen, saying, "Et genus et formam *regina* Pecunia donat;" and, looking at the existing state of things around us, we cannot any of us get rid of the idea that after all money is the great power which rules the world.

But to return to the Rothschilds. When Meyer Amschel Rothschild first saw the light of day, the Jews, though no longer tied to a single spot in London, were literally in fetters at Frankfort. In 1743 the "Jews' lane" was a prison, guarded at either end with heavy chains, which were fastened every evening by the watchmen, and also were kept closed on all Sundays, Feast Days, and Holy Days. Out of this pent-up district, only some 300 yards long, the wretched inhabitants were not allowed to stir under penalty of death. "No Jew," says Mr. Martin, "was allowed under any pretence to live beyond the limits of the 'Judengasse;' a rule which compelled the poor outcasts either to raise their dark sunless dwellings higher and higher with each succeeding generation, or else to hide themselves away in deep cellars underground. Such were the early surroundings that greeted the birth of the world-famed banking dynasty." Shame on Christians, indeed, that such should have been the case; but it only proves the truth of Byron's sneer,

> "Christians have burnt each other, quite persuaded
> That all th' Apostles would have done as they did."

At the age of eleven young Rothschild lost his parents, and had to begin the battle of life singlehanded. After a few years' schooling, one fine morning he packed up all his worldly goods on his shoulders, and with a stout stick in his hand walked to Hanover. Here he fortunately found a place as clerk to a small banker and money changer. By dint of extreme parsimony he managed to save a little out of his small salary, and with this capital in hand he returned to Frankfort in the year of grace 1775, just over a hundred years ago. I wonder if the house of Rothschild remembered to keep in the year 1873 their founder's centenary.

Meyer Amschel now took to himself a wife, and established himself as a broker and money-lender in the Juden-gasse, joining with his other business a little money-lending on a small scale. As a skilful collector of, and an honest dealer in old coins and other rarities, he soon gained some local fame, and many a virtuoso would look in upon him at his shop, No. 148, over the door of which he hung out his sign, the " Red Shield." which in allusive heraldry denoted " Roth Schild."

Among the connoisseurs with whom he was thus brought into connection was William, the Landgrave of Hesse Cassel, afterwards known as William I, Elector of Hesse. In those troubled and dangerous times, when the first Napoleon was making every town in Europe quake, the Landgrave no doubt was often glad to dispose of stray family jewels for a supply of the needful, and possibly to borrow a few hundreds on personal security in order to pay the more pressing of his creditors. Thus intimate relations were established between the Landgrave and the once poor clerk of Hanover: and so in 1796, when the French troops marched on Frankfort, the owner of the "Red Shield" had time to put his "little all" safe within the sheltering walls of the Landgrave's Schloss at Cassel—a service which the Jew banker was able to return with interest ten years later. The event is worth noticing, as marking the starting point of the career of the house of Rothschild.

As a rule, bombardments are not very fortunate in their consequences; but the bombardment of Frankfort by Kleber, in 1796, was not without its advantages to the Jews at least. The "Ghetto" of that city was knocked nearly to pieces, and the Jews were thenceforth allowed, as a special favour and privilege, to rent houses among their Christian brethren. The "Red Shield" was transferred to a better part of the city, and its owner was appointed banker to the Landgrave and his court.

This led to an event which proved the turning point of the fortunes of the Rothschilds. In 1806, the Landgrave was driven from his throne by Napoleon, who wanted the territory in order to consolidate the kingdom of Westphalia, which he had recently conferred on his brother, Jerome. In his hurry to "pack up and be off," William had no time to secure his cash, which he was only too glad to leave in the hands of his banker, though probably he had his misgivings as to seeing it again. Safer, however, he thought in the hands of Meyer Amschel, his *Hof-agent*, than in the hands of the merry King of Westphalia. The sum amounted to just a quarter of million of English pounds. The *Hof-agent*, however, was equal to the crisis; he saw how to take care of the money, and to make it bring in a good return also; and at a time when gold was worth from 12 to 20 per cent., and when all who were "hard up" were forced to mortgage their lands and houses, he saw that it only required a cool head and sound judgment to turn the capital over with advantage. The result was that in six years he had nearly quadrupled the original sum in his hands, and when he died, in 1812, he was found to be worth a million sterling.

Shortly after this event happened the battle of Leipzic, and on the re-establishment of peace the Landgrave was restored to his estates and his petty royalty. He had not been many days at his palace when he received a call from the eldest son of his departed *Hof-agent*, who handed him the quarter of a million which six years before he had left with Meyer Amschel. The Landgrave was overjoyed at the sight of his cash, and feeling that he could not pay too much honour to such honesty and probity, dubbed young Rothschild a knight on the spot. At the Congress of Vienna, which he attended shortly afterwards, he was loud in his praises of the Rothschilds; and the result was that the other crowned heads of Europe were anxious to secure the services of so trustworthy a banker, who, no doubt, was equally ready to do for any one of them what he had done for the Landgrave, namely, take care of their money and repay it without interest.

Meyer Amschel Rothschild left ten children— five daughters and five sons—who by their father's will were bidden to enter into partnership, binding themselves under the most solemn promises to be true to each other, and to keep the great Hof Agency business in their own hands, without allowing strangers to interfere with it. They were to establish different branches of the central bank at Frankfort, in London, Paris, and the other capitals of Europe, and thus to keep each other well informed as to all the centres of politics and business.

"Anselm, the eldest son, was to be the head of the firm," says Mr. Martin, "directing all its operations, and, if necessary, controlling the actions of his brothers. However, this arrangement was not strictly carried out, for, though

Anselm remained all his life the nominal head, yet his third brother (Nathan) inherited the largest share of his father's spirit, and became the real chief of the house." It was this Nathan Meyer Rothschild, I may here remark, who eventually settling in London, was naturalised in England, was created a Baron of the Austrian Empire, and became the father of Sir Anthony Rothschild, the first English baronet of the family. I must now pass on to his history.

Born in September, 1777, he left his home at Frankfort in 1798, at the age of twenty-one, and opened a small place of business as a banker and money-lender at Manchester, which city he is said to have reached with £84 in his pocket after paying his travelling expenses. By dint of shrewdness, perseverance, and self-denial, however, he had so successfully conducted his operations that he came from Manchester to London with a capital of £200,000 at his command. He engaged largely in speculations in the public funds, a safe step considering the supply of information which he received from abroad; and as he realized vast profits, his £200,000 speedily added a fresh " 0 " to it.

The next part of the story I will leave Mr. Martin to tell in his own words:

"An instance of young Rothschild's sound calculation, and which proved an event of the greatest importance in his successful career, was his first transaction with the British Government. In 1810, during the period when the fortunes of the Peninsular War seemed most doubtful, some drafts of Wellington, amounting in the aggregate to a considerable sum, came over to this country, and there was no money to meet them in the Exchequer. Nathan Rothschild, calculating with habitual shrewdness the chances of England's victory in her great contest against the arms of France, purchased the bills at a considerable discount, and, having made them over to the Government at par, furnished the money for redeeming them. It was a splendid speculation in every respect, and, according to Nathan's own confession, one of the best he ever made. Henceforth, the Ministry entered into frequent and intimate relations with the new Hebrew banker, who fully realised the pecuniary advantages which this connection brought him. Every piece of early news which he obtained brought him the gain of thousands at the Stock Exchange, the manipulation of which he had mastered to an unexampled degree. Soon, however, even the information which the resources of the Government furnished him was deemed insufficient by the enterprising speculator, and he set to originate means of his own for obtaining news far more perfect than those at the service of the Government. For this purpose he organized a staff of active agents, whose duty it was to follow in the wake of the continental armies, and to send daily, or, if necessary, hourly reports of the most important movements, successes or defeats, in ciphers hidden under the wings of carrier pigeons. To the breed of these pigeons Nathan Rothschild attended with the greatest care, and often paid large sums for birds of superior strength and swiftness."

But he was not always content with the news sent at second hand through pigeons, a mode of transit always liable to be intercepted by a stray shot from a Cockney's or a schoolboy's gun. Occasionally he would make his way to the Continent himself, in order to note matters with his own eye. For instance, when Napoleon returned from Elba, his anxiety for the pecuniary prospects of the house led him to Belgium, where he followed events, moving in the wake of the army under Wellington. Eager to glean the latest intelligence, he even ventured on the edge of the battle of Waterloo, where he witnessed the defeat of the French from the high ground in front of the château of Hougonmont.

As soon as the fate of the battle was decided,

Nathan Rothschild rode as fast as his horse could carry him to Brussels, where a chaise was in waiting to take him on to Ostend, which he reached at daybreak on June 19th. The sea was rough, and he had therefore some little difficulty in getting a boat across; but a brave fisherman agreed to peril his life for the sum of £80, and the same night he was safe in Dover harbour. Posting on to London, and sleeping in the chaise, he reached the City early on the 20th, and at ten o'clock was leaning against his accustomed pillar at the Stock Exchange. He looked solemn and anxious; and whispered to some of his acquaintances a rumour that Marshal Blücher and Wellington had suffered a defeat, and that Napoleon was master of the field and of the day.

The news spread like wildfire; down, of course, went the funds; Nathan Rothschild's known agents sold with the rest, but his unknown and secret agents bought still more largely, picking up every bit of scrip that they could lay hands on till the following day. On the afternoon of that day (the 21st) the real news reached London—the news of the fall of Napoleon. Radiant with joy, Nathan Rothschild was the first to inform his friends on the Stock Exchange of the happy event. The funds rose as fast as they had fallen—perhaps even a little faster—

THE RISE OF THE ROTHSCHILDS.   261

and no sooner were the official returns of the battle made known to the world, than it was found that the house of Rothschild had netted a million by the transaction. Enough: the foundations of the monetary dynasty of that house were now secure.

Having thus gained their first couple of millions, the Rothschilds soon found honour and dignities showered thick upon them. The Emperor of Austria raised all the five brothers to the rank of hereditary nobles; and seven years later granted them patents of dignity as barons. And as for Nathan, his career after Waterloo was as prosperous as it had been before. "He made money," says Mr. Martin, " even by speculations which turned out bad; for instance, by the English loan of twelve millions, for which he became responsible in 1819, and which fell to a discount: but this did not happen until Nathan had relieved himself of all responsibility. His greatest successes, however, were in foreign loans, which he was the first to make popular in England, by introducing the habit of paying in the London market the dividends which previously had been paid abroad, and by fixing the rate in sterling money."

From about the year 1819 the transactions of the brothers Rothschild came to be spread over the whole civilised world, and Nathan negotiated in person or by proxy loans with the Czar of Russia and with the South American Republics, and drove his bargains with the Pope of Rome and the Sultan of Turkey; and yet, while dealing with these world-wide matters, he could calculate to a sixpence what each of his clerk's wages should amount to; and he took care that they should never be overpaid a penny, even when he was himself entertaining at his table peers, bishops, and even Princes of the Blood Royal. And yet he was not happy. His utter want of education rendered him quite unfit to enjoy the pleasures of London society, and at the same time exposed him to the shafts of satire. He was constantly made the subject of caricatures, which nettled and pained him to a degree; and he was constantly in receipt of *billets doux*, sent by the post anonymously, which contained threats of assassination unless he sent large sums of money to the writers.

In the year 1831 Nathan Rothschild did a stroke of business which, while it brought him and his house immense profits, also heaped upon them not a little obloquy, freely expressed in many English and foreign newspapers. It is well known that the supply of mercury is exceedingly limited, being almost entirely drawn from two mines, those of Almaden, in Spain, and of Idria, near Adelsberg, in Illyria. The mines of Almaden, which were known to the Greeks 700 years before Christ, and which furnished £700,000 annually to Rome during the Imperial era, fell somewhat into neglect, on account of the Napoleonic wars at the commencement of the present century, so that the Spanish Government derived less profit from them than formerly. Under these circumstances, when the Ministers of His Catholic Majesty were hard up for funds in 1831, they entertained the application of Nathan to furnish them with a loan, on condition of the Almaden mines being made over to him for a number of years as security. The bargain was struck, and the House of Rothschild entered into possession of the mines, commencing the business by immediately doubling the price of Almaden mercury. The commercial world, much astonished at this step, addressed itself to Idria; and then it was discovered that the mines of Idria had passed likewise very quietly into the hands of Nathan Rothschild, who had settled of course the price of the mercury on the same scale as that of Almaden. By this little transaction the House of Rothschild obtained a complete monopoly in the sale of mercury, and Nathan was able to fix the price of the article, indispensable for many purposes, at his counting-house in St Swithin's-lane. This clever stroke of business—as profitable as it was clever—had one notable consequence for the sick and suffering of all nations. Mercurial preparations, largely employed in medicine, are at present no more manufactured from the pure metal as obtained from the mines, but from the refuse of other articles containing quicksilver, such as the foil of old mirrors and looking glasses. It would be interesting, if the statistics were to be obtained, to calculate how many pounds sterling the House of Rothschild made by the little mercury business, and how many persons suffered in consequence of bad mercurial medicines.

The grand secret and guiding principle which has ensured the continuance of the prosperity of the House of Rothschild has been the unity which has attended the co-partnership of its members, so strongly enjoined as a duty on his children by its founder, Meyer Amschel, as he lay on his death-bed. It is, after all, but a realisation of the truth of the fable of the bundle of sticks, a fresh example of the saying that "union is strength." To cement and to continue this bond of union, Nathan conceived the further idea of linking the family still closer together by the intermarriage of the broker's children. Accordingly in 1836 he summoned a meeting of the family at Frankfort to discuss, and, if possible, to ratify the question. His advice was followed, and the congress broke up with an arrangement for the marriage of the eldest son of Nathan Rothschild with the eldest daughter of his brother Charles.

Nathan had arrived at Frankfort in the May of that year in perfect health and spirits, and he took part in the religious ceremonies which attended the wedding of his son and his niece on the 15th of June. Next day, however, he was taken ill; he grew rapidly worse, and it was suggested that his physician in London, Dr. Travers, should be summoned; but the travelling expenses of a London physician to Germany were too heavy for the purse of a Rothschild, and a cheap medical adviser from the city of Frankfort was called in. Under his hands poor Nathan Rothschild got worse and worse, grew delirious, and talked only of his pounds, his notes, and his thalers, and on the 28th he died.

Early on the morning of the next day a sportsman, looking out for birds on the downs near Brighton, shot a pigeon, which, when picked up, proved to be one of the well-known carriers of the House of Rothschild. It carried no letter under its wings, but only a small bit of paper on which were written the words *Il est mort,* with two initials. Who the *il* was there could be no doubt. Next day there was almost a panic on the Stock Exchange, and a great fall in the funds—greater even than that which occurred on the death of Sir Thomas Baring.

The remains of Nathan Rothschild were brought over to England, placed in a sumptuously gilded coffin, and buried with great pomp and state in the Jewish cemetery at the East-end of London, his hearse being followed by a train of mourning carriages nearly a mile in length, and the cavalcade included not only the Lord Mayor and Sheriffs of London, but also the Austrian, Russian, Prussian, and Neapolitan ambassadors. Verily, if money be not a king, it sometimes has a royal following.

The fortune left by the head of the family was variously estimated at three, six, and even ten millions. It is probable that the exact sum was never really known, as large sums had been made over to various members of his family in his lifetime. After declaring that he had an interest in all the houses conducted by his brothers on the Continent, he ordered that his four sons should join their uncles in carrying on the transactions—I suppose I must not call it "business"—of the house, and to each of his three daughters he left a paltry £100,000, forbidding them to marry without the consent of their mother and brothers. "This," as Mr Martin remarks, "was but a furtherance of the guiding thought of the latter part of his life, when he dreamed that he was destined to elevate his family into a distinct class or caste, equal to that of the Royal families of Europe, and all united in the close ties of blood alliance. Perhaps, at times, he even looked forward to the day when the house of the "Red Shield" should stand far higher than those of Hapsburg and Coburg, by the right of a power far higher and more stable than that of ancestry —the power of gold."

Such a dream, if Nathan Rothschild ever dreamed it, has not come true, nor does it seem likely ever now to be realized. Another generation has sprung up; the head of the English house is a baronet, and two of the Rothschilds have seats in Parliament; the Rothschilds now own Gunnersbury Park in Middlesex and Tring Park in Hertfordshire, and Mentmore in Buckinghamshire; and some of their handsome Jewish daughters have exchanged their Israelitish maiden names for Christian surnames.* The

---

* Hannah, sister of Baron Rothschild and of Sir A. Rothschild, married in 1839 the late Right Hon. Henry Fitzroy, M.P. for Lewes, brother of the late Lord Southampton; and

caste is broken in upon; the wall of severance is no longer standing; and Jewish wealth has now become in the matrimonial market an article of exchange for Christian blood and noble titles. May the blending of the two principles be happy in its results!

more recently a daughter of Baron Rothschild, of Mentmore has entered the bonds of matrimony after the Christian rite with the Hon. Mr. Yorke, a younger son of the Earl of Hardwicke.

AN EPISODE IN THE HOUSE OF HARLEY.

AMONG our "great families," whose names are coeval with the Norman Conquest, whose heads in the days of the last Stuart sovereign "held the realm in pawn," are the Harleys, who for a century and a half after the extinction of the heroic House of Vere enjoyed the dignity of Earls of Oxford, and one of the last of whom figured in his day as a merchant, Alderman, and Lord Mayor of London. The old peerage-makers tell us that that the family "can be traced to a period antecedent to the Conquest," at which date its position was so eminent that it forked, like the Harcourts, into two rival branches, one on each side of the English Channel, bearing their original name of Harlai in France.

We find that in or about the reign of our Edward II., a certain knight, Sir Robert de

Harley, married Margaret, eldest daughter and co-heiress (with her sister, Elizabeth, wife of Sir Richard de Cornwall, Son of Richard, Earl of Cornwall, King of the Romans, brother of Henry II.) of Sir Bryan de Brampton, in virtue of which marriage he gained the magnificent estate and noble castle of Brampton Bryan, near Ludlow, which has continued down to this day in the hands of his descendants. And Sir Bernard Burke tells us that his grandson, Sir John Harley, of Brampton Bryon, received the honour of knighthood from Edward IV. on the field of battle. From him, eighth or ninth in direct lineal descent, was Sir Robert Harley, of Brampton Bryan, M.P., for Herefordshire, Master of the Mint under Charles I., a man whose name is worthy of remembrance, if for no other reason, because he refused to coin money at the Royal Mint in the Tower with any other die than that of his Royal Master. For this offence he was deposed by the Parliament, and he does not appear to have lived to see the Restoration. His wife, Lady Brilliana Harley, was a niece of Dorothy, daughter of Sir John Tracy, of Toddington, Gloucestershire, and sister of Mary, wife of Sir Horace Vere, Lord Vere of Tilbury, through which union the Harleys became allied with the Veres, ancient Earls of Oxford, whose name is

—or rather was for twenty generations—a synonym for the very flower of English nobility. Lady Brilliana was almost as celebrated for her defence of Brampton Castle, when invested by the Parliamentary forces in 1643, as was Lady Blanche Arundell—the Wiltshire heroine of the same period—for her defence of Wardour Castle, near Salisbury. Her story is rather a touching one; for although she had held the place for seven weeks against her assailants, she forced them to raise the siege, yet she died a few weeks afterwards, her end being hastened by her annoyance and grief at the siege. After her death the Roundheads returned to their work, and laid siege a second time to the castle, which they took, and then burned to the ground. A mass of noble ruins still remains to show what the size of the castle must have been in the days of its splendour.

The son of the owners of Brampton Castle, Sir Edward Harley, was a member of the Parliament that called back Charles II. to his throne, and was appointed Governor of Dunkirk in reward of his father's services and losses in the Royal cause. His eldest son, Robert Harley, successively Speaker of the House of Commons, Secretary of State, and Chancellor of the Exchequer, was created Earl of Oxford and Mortimer in 1711, and four years later was impeached and committed to the Tower. His public trial and his acquittal on the charge of high treason in the reign of George I, are matters well known to every school-boy or school-girl. His son and successor, the second earl, was the gleaner and editor of the valuable collection of historical documents which is known to scholars as the *Harleian Miscellany*, and which was purchased from his widow for the British Museum. The third earl was his cousin, also Edward, of whom little more need be said than that he married and had four sons, of whom the eldest reigned as a peer in his stead, the second was Bishop of Hereford, and the fourth a prebendary of Worcester, while his third son Thomas, was sent into the city to make his fortune, or at all events to push his way. The story of this Thomas Harley I now come to tell.

Athough the son and the brother of an Earl of Oxford, yet this gentleman shared the fate which is so common among the younger sons even of titled parents, namely, that of having to begin the world with but a very small supply of money. Young Harley was educated at the school at Westminster, but it is not on record that on leaving his father's house at Westminster he walked through Temple Bar and journeyed eastwards into the City of London proper, with only the conventional half-a-crown in his pocket which usually figures on these occasions. Indeed, it is not at all certain that he went through Temple Bar at all, for even at that date there were more ways than one into the heart of London. One way, at all events, was by the river, not in a steamer, but in a hired wherry or his father's private barge.

It so happened that his father's steward, who had made some pickings out of the Harley estates, was possessed of a very pretty daughter, one Anna—or as she was called "Nanny"—Bangham, and she became the fair goddess of his destiny. She was her father's heiress, was known to have a good fortune "looming in the future," and her father, plain Edward Bangham, thought that none would have a better right to share it with her than one of his master's sons. The fates were propitious; young Thomas Harley "popped the question" which has made (or marred) so many men before him and after him. Old Bangham was quite as willing as his fair daughter to say "yes;" so the affair was soon settled, and her money too. He received with "Nanny" a handsome fortune, with which, at the ripe age of twenty-two, the Honourable Thomas Harley commenced business in the wine trade, and became a citizen of London, resolving mentally, no doubt, to sit one day in the civic chair.

Time went on. Harley prospered in his business, and the fact of his having a "handle" to his name, we may be sure, did not stand in his way among the good people who worship Mammon much, but "blue blood" even more, to the east of Temple Bar. Ten years after his marriage, and his start in business, namely, in 1762, we find him chosen an Alderman of London, and in the same year one of the members of the City, having succeeded to the seat vacated by its late respected representative, Sir John Barnard. He served as Sheriff of London in 1764, and became Lord Mayor in 1768.

During his shrievalty he made himself famous, though not perhaps popular in the City, by seizing the emblems of the "boot" and "petticoat," which the mob were burning in the street opposite the Mansion House, in mockery of Lord Bute and the Princess Dowager, while the Sheriffs were busily engaged, on their parts, in burning the *North Briton*, the paper of John Wilkes. The people in the mob were throwing copies of the paper about in sport and fun, when one of them—probably carrying inside of it a handful of dirt or a stone—was hurled through the front window of Mr. Sheriff Harley's chariot, shattering the glass. This caused an alarm, and the Sheriffs retired, with sound discretion, to the Mansion House. Some few of the ring-leaders of

the mob were arrested, and brought before the
Lord Mayor; but it turned out to be a "storm in
a tea-cup," and it appeared that no danger to the
Constitution was designed or contemplated by
the populace, though angry with the civic mag-
nates.

A proposal being made to offer a vote of thanks
to the Sheriffs, for discharging their duty on this
not very difficult or critical occasion, was nega-
tived by the Lord Mayor himself, who stated
publicly that he did not consider the affair as
"sufficiently important for a public and solemn
acknowledgment, which," he declared with em-
phasis, "ought to follow only the most eminent
exertions of duty."

For this refusal—it is almost incredible—the
Duke of Bedford, in his place in the House of
Lords moved that the Mayor and Corporation of
London should be "ordered to attend at the bar
to answer for their conduct;" while another duke,
His Grace of Richmond, in seconding the motion,
took to himself and his leader great credit for
not moving a formal address to His Majesty,
urging him to "deprive the City of its charter."
Lord Mansfield, who had, fortunately, enjoyed a
legal instead of a ducal education, with great
good sense and coolness, explained the matter in
all its bearings, to the satisfaction of the House,

and in the end prevailed upon the two dukes to withdraw a motion which could not be justified upon any principle of reason, law, or liberty.

For his service on this occasion, however, Mr. Harley was sworn a Privy Councillor, so that he could style himself "Right Honourable" long before he attained the honours of the mayoralty.* But in proportion as he gained favour at Court, he lost it in the City; and in consequence he was thrown out of Parliament at the next election, and was afterwards unsuccessful in his candidature for Herefordshire, in which county it might be thought the Harley interest would have been all-powerful. At length, in 1775, on the occasion of Mr. Foley being raised to the peerage, when the memory of his shrievalty had passed away, the farmers and cider-makers of Herefordshire thought better of the affair, and sent him as their representative to St. Stephen's; and he continued to hold his seat for a quarter of a century or more.

There is little or nothing to say with respect to Mr. Harley's mayoralty, except that it was

---

* It is stated by Mr. Sylvanus Urban in the obituary notice of Mr. Harley in the *Gentleman's Magazine* for 1804, that this honour had never before been conferred on any of his predecessors in the mayoralty from the days of Sir William Walworth.

uneventful, and that at the close of it he had won back part at least of that capricious and fleeting substance called public favour.

"It cannot be denied," observes a writer in the *Gentleman's Magazine*, who was eminently acquainted with the City politics of seventy years ago, "that in consequence of the peculiar temper of the times, and the imperious duty thence frequently imposed on him of firmly resisting the headstrong course of popular licentiousness, the conduct of Mr. Harley was frequently exposed, as might have been expected, to obloquy and misrepresentation. A strong instance of this was afforded in the case of the press-warrants in 1770 and the following year. As he never wanted popular favour, nor practised those disingenuous artifices by which the fleeting applause of a giddy multitude is too often successfully pursued, it was not in the transient popularity of a day that he sought the reward of his exertions, but in the approbation of his own conscience, and, next to that, in the well-founded and permanent praise of those whose praise he justly valued. *Laudari a laudatis* was ever the object of his ambition. At this distance of time, however, when the ebullitions of popular fury have, together with their effects, long since happily subsided in this kingdom, and when the lamentable consequences of uncontrolled democratic frenzy have been so abundantly exemplified in our eyes in the total ruin and desolation of neighbouring States, it will hardly be thought to derogate from Mr. Harley's public character when we state that, in the vigilant discharge of his official duties he was frequently exposed to insult and opposition from a lawless and irritated mob; that, in burning *The North Briton,* while he was Sheriff, in 1764, he was violently and tumultuously assaulted; that, on more than one occasion during his mayoralty he encountered, with a characteristic coolness, and with the most determined intrepidity, very serious personal danger; and that when afterwards, in 1770, he was going up with a number of fellow-citizens to present a loyal address to his Sovereign on the birth of a princess, he was even forcibly torn from his chariot, and prevented from proceeding to St. James's. It is more pleasant to relate that in later and better times a very different sentiment had universally prevailed in the metropolis; and, it is a fact that even his former political opponent, Mr. Wilkes himself, who will probably be as little suspected of partiality in this as of want of discernment in any instance, has frequently been heard to bear honourable testimony, in the latter years of his life, to the merits of Mr.

Harley's public conduct, declaring it to have been at all times uniform, manly, and consistent."

He also continued to draw a good income from his business as a merchant, to which he eventually added that of a banker, and prospered in his double capacity. In conjunction with another gentleman, named Drummond—I believe, his son-in-law—he had at one time a contract for supplying the army in America with foreign gold —a contract out of which the two are said to have realized a fortune of more than half a million. With the proceeds of this contract he bought a fine property at Berrington, near Leominster, on which he built a sumptuous residence, in fact a sort of palace. But, partly owing to the extravagance of his style of living, and partly in consequence of some extensive failures, "there was in his banking-house in 1797," says a contemporary writer, "something like a hesitation of payment." With respect to this event, "Sylvanus Urban" says: "At a period when this critical and even awful state of public affairs had given a shock to public credit, which was felt not only by the most respectable commercial houses throughout the kingdom, but also in some measure by the Bank of England itself, Mr. Harley determined at once to relinquish all his commercial concerns. The most liberal and friendly offers of pecuniary aid, he had declined in the most disinterested manner; and having made a voluntary assignment of all his real and personal property (should it be wanting) for the honourable payment of all his partnership demands, he had soon the heartfelt satisfaction of seeing them all discharged in their fullest extent, both as to principal and interest, a proof of his uprightness and integrity which raised him even higher than before in the estimation of his fellow-citizens."

Even after this momentary failure, though advanced in years, he was strongly urged to allow himself to be put forward as a candidate for the chamberlainship of the City, when vacant by the death of Mr. Wilkes; but he declined the proposal, in a "manly and feeling address" to the Livery, in which he stated among other reasons that, in event of such a vacancy, he was pledged to support the individual who in point of fact was elected to the post. On quitting the representation of the City in 1774, he issued another address to the Liverymen of London, "strongly marked by that manly steadiness and consistency of character, that clear discernment and vigour of intellect, by which he was at all times distinguished in public and private life." Mr. Harley spent the last few years of his life in retirement.

He was for some years before his death "the Father of the City," and he drew a salary of £300 a-year from the civic funds as governor of the Irish Society. His wife died in 1798, and he followed her to the grave in 1804. His biographer, in the columns of the *Gentleman's Magazine*, records the fact that, down to near the end of his life, he continued the vigilant and active discharge of his civic duties in the metropolis, retaining to the time of his death his alderman's gown, and having become by the death of Mr. Alsop, in 1785, the "Senior or Father of the City." He left five daughters, his co-heirs—two of whom married peers—but no son to succeed him; and, though the earldom of Oxford lived on till 1853, yet the male line of the ancient and noble House of Harley is now extinct; its memory, however, is embalmed in the name of Harley Street, so named after the celebrated author of the *Harleian Miscellany*, who is mentioned above as the second earl.

THE BAD LORD STOURTON.

THE noble House of Stourton is of great antiquity in Wiltshire, deriving its name from the village of Stourton—the town or ville upon the Stour—where its head held broad acres from a date before the Conquest down to the beginning of the Georgian era. That the Stourtons were men of note and of power at that early date is proved by the fact that Botolph de Stourton was one of the chief opponents of the Norman invader in the west, disputing every inch of ground against him, breaking down the sea walls of the Severn, guarding the land passages, and securing Glastonbury, so that he was able to dictate even to William the Conqueror the terms on which he would yield possession of the soil. From him descended a long line of knights, who fought for the Holy Sepulchre in their generations, and sought their mates among the Bassets, the Vernons, and the Berkeleys. One of this line, Sir John Stourton, a gallant warrior, and also a statesman, in the reign of Henry VI., was raised to the peerage in A.D. 1455 as Lord Stourton. His great-great-grandson, Charles, the seventh baron, however, sadly tarnished the family escutcheon by a deed of murder, which he expiated in the market-place at Salisbury.

This deed of violence took its origin in a strife arising out of those Forest Laws which were so cruel a source of oppression of our poorer classes in the Middle Ages. As Mrs. Crosse writes in "Once a Week:" "Every schoolboy knows that the tyranny of the early Norman kings was felt most keenly in their cruel exactions for the preservation of game. To kill beasts of the chase was as penal as the murder of a man. We can easily understand how stoutly our ancestors battled for the "Charta de Foresta," which was extorted with as much reluctance as the Magna Charta itself. Even when the laws had undergone a considerable amelioration, common persons keeping dogs within the limits of the forest were obliged to cut away the balls of their forefeet, to render them incapable of pursuing game or of hunting the deer. Great dissatisfaction arose from time to time in respect to the encroachments of the limits of the royal hunting grounds, and bad blood was produced between the great landowners and the yeomanry and tenantry on the other."

In order to see an example of the sad effects of the laws, I will ask my readers to accompany me to the forest of Selwood, which lies on the borders of Wiltshire and Somersetshire, in the direction between Salisbury and Bath.

This tract of land, pleasantly diversified by a succession of hills and valleys, must have been very picturesque in the days when as yet it was not cut up by modern "improvements," and what is known as "high farming." These fair lands, some twelve miles long by five in breadth, were in due course of time "disafforested," not, however, without a great deal of opposition from those who were directly interested in keeping them up as a "chase," and who preferred the interests of their horses and dogs to those of a prosperous and contented peasantry. But there are two sides to every question; and the whirligig of time brought it about in the course of a couple of centuries--I do not stop here to explain how—that the yeomen and cottagers obtained a prescriptive right to pasture their cattle on the outlying parts of the forest of Selwood; and of course the lower orders had a personal interest in preserving its glades from encroachment by lords and squires. Again to quote the words of Mrs Crosse: "Towards the close of the reign of Henry the Eighth the nobles began to slice off pieces of the outlying wastes and commons, inclosing them for their own pastures and parks. A belief in the rights of the soil is so inherent in human nature that it is not surprising that the people rose and resisted to the very death this encroachment on their privileges. They were first despoiled of their lands by the king, and, now that the forest laws had fallen into desuetude, they were robbed of their pasturage by the nobles. The evil had attained to such a height that in 1549, a proclamation was issued by Edward VI. to restrain certain nobles and gentry from inclosing the commons and converting them into their own pastures and parks, and commanding that all ground that had been thus inclosed should be thrown open on a certain day, under heavy penalties." But the good intentions of this order were disregarded by the great landowners; and the result was that the cottagers assembled and raised tumults throughout the district, breaking down the fences which inclosed the parks which Lord Herbert and Lord Stourton had carved out from the lands which, though illegally, they had looked upon as "waste." The Crown on more than one occasion sent down a commission to quell these disturbances; but one of these at all events was not destined to pass away without bloodshed.

In the district of which I write is a parish called Kilmington, and in it lived a yeoman family named Hartgill, between whom and Lord Stourton there was evidently "no love lost." In fact, both the father and the son had taken active measures to oppose his lordship's arbitrary attempts to inclose the adjacent lands; but Lord Stourton would not yield, and no doubt felt all the more sorely wounded because his opponent was a man of only middle class birth and parentage. The Hartgills sent up a memorial to the Privy Council, and in the course of a week or two a royal mandate came from London, a scarlet-coated messenger from Whitehall, desiring his lordship to desist from an inclosure he had commenced, and to avoid giving occasion for further "misliking" among his neighbours.

At this time his lordship, who had married a sister of the Duke of Northumberland, happened to die; but the quarrel between the Stourtons and the Hartgills was not buried in his grave—it was taken up with all possible bitterness by his son and successor Charles, the seventh lord, the individual already mentioned.

A few years passed on, but apparently the strife between the lord of the great house and the yeoman's family was as lively as ever. At Whitsuntide, 1556, it appears that Lord Stourton came over from Stourton to Kilmington, with the pretended grievance that the Hartgills had been hunting with horses and dogs in his park. With him came a large band of retainers, armed with guns and bows, and evidently bent on mischief. We catch a glimpse of the rough manners of the forefathers of the yeomen of Wilts and Somerset when we read that the Hartgills, on hearing of his lordship's approach, retreated into the parish church of Kilmington for safety. One of the old man's sons, however, John by name, ran back to his father's homestead, in order to fetch some staves, some bows and arrows, and other weapons of offence and defence. As he ran across, several arrows were shot at him by Lord Stourton's men, but these happily missed their aim. Several of the villagers now came up to aid the Hartgills, and actually drove the Stourtonites from the churchyard and its precincts, while the old people with their servants took refuge in the tower of the church, and laid in a supply of bread and meat in order to stand a siege.

One can easily imagine the face of the elder Hartgill as he peered warily out of the church window, and, after thanking his son for the supply of food, bade him go up with all speed to London, to lay the facts of the case before the Queen and her Council at Whitehall.

Scarce was young John Hartgill out of sight, when Lord Stourton and his "men of war" returned to the churchyard, keeping the old people shut up in the dark belfry of the tower in a pretty state of nervous alarm. One of them, however, went off to the yeoman's defenceless farm-house, and took out of the stables old Hartgill's favourite riding horse, valued at eight pounds, and shot him with a cross-bow, in sight of his owner, giving out that the latter had been seen on it hunting in his lordship's park.

Meantime the son returned from London, having so far succeeded in his mission that at his request the Lords of the Council sent down a commission, with the high sheriff of Somerset at its head, ordering Lord Stourton to appear before them. His lordship was, therefore, obliged to swallow his rage, and make a journey to London in custody of the sheriff. On reaching Whitehall he was committed to the Fleet Prison, to which no doubt he was conveyed by the old "silent highway" of the river Thames. In all probability, however, as being the brother-in-law of the Duke of Northumberland, he speedily found a means of escape—perhaps by the use of a "silver key;" for, if I may believe the account of this affair as given by the antiquary Strype, he was soon back at Kilmington, harassing the Hartgills with all the malice of which he was capable.

And so matters stood for a year or two, during which I suppose that the Hartgills came down from their fastness in the church tower, and went about their business as if nothing strange had happened. But it is clear that the Stourtons would not let them remain in quiet. On the accession of Mary, the Hartgills and their fellow-yeomen appear to have presented a fresh petition, asking either for protection from their tyranny, or redress against their violence, for the Council at Whitehall again called the brawlers before them. Lord Stourton now made all sorts of promises of good behaviour, vowing that if any of the Hartgills' cattle or horses had been detained at Stourton House, they had only to come and fetch them, and they should have them freely and readily. But they soon learnt not to "put their trust in princes;" for as they were going to the great house they were attacked by several of his lordship's men, who attacked and wounded John Hartgill, and left him for dead in the road.

This affair had now grown so serious as to have attracted the attention of the Court of the Star Chamber, to whom, we read, "the matter appeared so heinously base on the Lord Stourton's side, that he was fined in a certain sum, to be paid over to the Hartgills." Besides this, his lordship was a second time committed as a prisoner to the Fleet. But fines and imprisonments had no weight with him. By hook or by crook he again contrived to effect his escape out of "durance vile," this time, however, giving a bond in £2000 to return when called upon to appear, and expressing a wish to settle the quarrel between himself and his old enemies by a money payment, and desiring the Hartgills to fix upon a place where they should receive the fine. Strype tells us that "the latter received his errand, but were in much doubt to adventure themselves," and not without good reason, as we shall see presently.

The rest of the story shall be told as condensed by Mrs. Crosse from old Strype's quaint and circumstantial narrative: "At length a meeting was arranged at Kilmington Church, and at ten of the clock one cold January morning Lord Stourton came, true to his appointment. But there came with him such a conclave of men on horseback and men on foot, that the Hartgills were in great dread. The open space near the church was nigh filled with this concourse, consisting of fifteen of Lord Stourton's own men, sundry of his tenants, besides several gentlemen and justices, to the number of about sixty persons in all. His lordship went into the church house, which was about forty paces distant, and thence sent word to the Hartgills, who were sheltering themselves under the sacred roof, ' that they must come out, for the church was no place to talk of worldly matters ;' whereupon they adventured themselves, coming within twenty paces, old Hartgill, after due salutation, saying, ' My lord, I see many of mine enemies about your lordship, therefore I am much afraid to come any nearer.' Upon this the company said, ' they durst promise all they had, they should have no bodily hurt.' Upon this comfort they approached to my lord's person. Lord Stourton then discoursed upon the reason which had brought them together, saying that if they would come into the church house he would pay them the money. But the Hartgills refused to go into any covered place, the church excepted.

"At this refusal there was much demur and talking, but some one present thought good that a table should be set upon the open green, which was done accordingly. Lord Stourton laid thereupon a cap-case and a purse, as though he intended to make payment; and calling unto the two Hartgills, he said that the council had ordered him to pay them a certain sum of money, which they should have every penny; 'but marry, he would first know them to be true men.' This was the watchword, which was no sooner said than Lord Stourton laid hands on William Hartgill, adding, 'I arrest you of felony.' Immediately ten or twelve of his own men surrounded the Hartgills and thrust them violently into the church house. Here his lordship produced 'two bands of inkle' which he had in readiness, and he caused his men to bind them with the same. He took from them their purses with his own hands, and finding afterwards a turquoise in one, gave it to Lady Stourton. When John Hartgill was bound he gave him a blow on his face, Sir James FitzJames and Chaffin looking on. At this moment young Hartgill's wife, no doubt alarmed at the commotion, rushed into the church house, encountering Lord Stourton at the door. He spurred and kicked at her, making a great rent in her hosen with his spur, and finally gave her such a blow with his sword between the head and neck that she fell backwards as though dead, and for three hours the company had much ado to keep life in her.' Such is the extraordinary account of the illegal arrest of two unoffending gentlemen, made in the presence of so many persons, that one is surprised that a feeling of common humanity did not come to rescue the oppressed."

But the worst part of the story remains to be told. Lord Stourton, having kept the Hartgills all day without food or drink, conveyed them bound as his prisoners to a house on his estate, called Bonhams, where he sent for two "justices of the peace" to examine them!—on what ground or charge is not stated. The so-called "justices" were probably creatures of his own, for we find that their examination ended in nothing but an order that they should be "losed of their bonds." The same night the prisoners were fetched away by some of Lord Stourton's minions, who, as it subsequently appeared in evidence, had orders to dispatch them if they made any resistance. Their destination now was a "close yard," adjoining the great house, where they were made to kneel down with their hands tied behind them, and were beaten till they were thought to be dead, "my lord in the the mean season standing at the gallery door, which was not a coyt's (quoit's) cast from the place." When the ruffians had done the job thus far, they wrapped up the bodies in their own gowns and carried them through a garden into the gallery, where they were joined by Lord Stourton himself, who carried a candle to show them the way, and who, when one of the dying men showed by a groan that life was not quite extinct, ordered his servant to cut their throats, " lest a French priest, who lay near, should hear them." The bodies were then cast into an underground chamber or dungeon, his lordship standing by with the candle in his hand.

One of the assassins, apparently with a softer heart than his fellow, said, " Oh, my lord, this is a pitiful sight. Had I thought what I now think before the thing was done, your whole land would not have won me to such an act." To this his wicked employer answered, " What, faint-hearted fool! is it any more than ridding the world of two knaves, that living were troublesome to God's law and man's? there is no more account to be made of them than the killing of two sheep!" And so they finished their hideous work of death by digging a grave for their victims, covering them first with earth and then with paving stones, while Lord Stourton kept walking up and down on the planks above, oftentimes calling to them to make speed, for that the night went away." But, though the night passed away and morning came, the hand of justice at length did not fail to overtake the wicked lord, who was arrested and carried to London to be judged for his foul crime. In January, 1556, he was committed to the Tower to await his trial, which took place on February 26 following, before the judges of the Council in Westminster Hall. It appears he entertained a hope that, being an adherent, nominally at least, of "the old religion," he would not be allowed by the Queen to suffer the extreme penalty of the law. But in this hope he was grievously mistaken. "The Queen and her Council," observes a writer of repute, "were greatly displeased at this, and willed process and judgment to proceed against him."

When called upon to make answer to the charge of wilful murder, he refused to plead, and would not open his mouth until he was threatened with being pressed to death if he remained silent. At last he pleaded guilty, and was sentenced to be hanged; four of his men also were sentenced to be hanged at the same time.

It may readily be supposed that these four poor wretches were turned off at St. Giles's Pound or at Tyburn tree; but the end of Lord Stourton himself was to be witnessed by the men of his own county. He was accordingly conveyed by easy stages by way of Hounslow, Staines, and Basingstoke to Salisbury, where he was executed on the 6th of March. The only favour shown to him was the permission that, in virtue of his rank, he should be throttled by a silken instead of a hempen cord. The market-place was the scene of his execution; and it is some comfort to learn that "he made great lamentation at his death for his wilful and impious deeds."

The memory of such a miscreant might well be allowed to pass away, and when he was buried in Salisbury Cathedral it would perhaps have been kinder to have erected no monument to mark the spot where he was laid. But in the north transept there is a tomb which is known as that of "the wicked Lord Stourton" by exhibiting the armorial bearings of the family in the shape of six circular openings, which represent the six springs which rose, and perhaps still rise, in the park at Stourton. The silken cord with which he suffered was suspended over his tomb for many years, till it rotted away and fell to pieces.

It is scarcely a matter of wonder that the

Stourton family should have long since sold their Wiltshire estates, and emigrated to Yorkshire, where their name is held deservedly in honour to the present day.

BENJAMIN, LORD BLOOMFIELD.

VERY many, if not most, of the members of our Peerage, both English and Irish, can boast with truth that they represent families of ancestral wealth and influence, or of historic note, or of brilliant achievements; and this is true to a far greater extent of the Peerage of Scotland, on the roll of which not a name appears that has not been adorned with a coronet for at least the best part of two centuries, while nearly all the pedigrees can be certified by the "Lyon" King of Arms at Edinburgh to extend back into the ages when the Stuarts had not yet added an English to their Scottish throne.

A few of the Irish families, however, have attained the honours of the peerage without any very great public services on the part of the first grantee, and without being able to boast of great wealth or noble ancestry. "My lord," said a wealthy squire and M.P., who lived in St. James's-place, to Lord Bute, or Lord Shelburne, or to some other Prime Minister of the last century, "I am very much inclined to support your measures in my place in Parliament, and to give you my vote and steady support; but I should be most glad and most obliged to you if, in return, you would go so far out of your way as to ask for me the permission of the Ranger (one of the royal dukes) to allow me the privilege of a private key which will admit me from my garden in St. James's-place into the Green Park without going round by way of the Palace." "I am sorry, sir," replied the Premier, with a benevolent smile, "that it is not in my power to oblige you in the precise manner in which you wish. The thing, I assure you, is an impossibility; and His Royal Highness has not only refused it to more than one applicant, but has desired me never to ask such a favour again. I will, however, with pleasure recommend you to His Majesty for an Irish peerage, if you feel inclined to accept the honour."

I do not know for certain whether the proffered Irish coronet was accepted by Mr. —— with the same readiness with which it was offered; but the story—which, by the way, is told with some variation by that old gossip, Sir Nathaniel Wraxall—may serve to show that Irish peerages were not held of very great account in London even in the good old days " when George the Third was king," and when the Legislative Union of 1800 had not been dreamed of as yet by the younger Pitt.

I am led into these remarks by way of introduction to the story of the rise and advancement of one plain Captain Benjamin Bloomfield of the Royal Artillery, to the dignity of " Lord Bloomfield, of Redwood, in the county of Tipperary, in the peerage of Ireland." It appears that the bestowal of this title was due in a very great measure to the concurrence of two or three fortunate accidents.

It so happened that a plain, untitled gentleman, "descended from an ancient family in Ireland," according to Sir Bernard Burke—albeit he omits all mention of his pedigree, " Ulster King of Arms " though he is—some sixty years ago held a commission in the Royal Artillery; and secondly, that he was at Brighton with his troop, when the Prince Regent had taken up his residence at the Pavilion, which he had recently built as a palace of pleasure. A third piece of gratuitous good fortune was to be found in the fact that the Captain was well known in Brighton as an accomplished player on the violoncello; and further by way of a fourth bit of luck his Royal Highness, in his idle and leisure hours, wanted some one who could accompany him on that instrument. Accordingly one day a message was sent to the barracks, requesting, or rather commanding, the presence of Capt. Bloomfield at the Pavilion. The summons was loyally and dutifully obeyed; Capt. Bloomfield put in an appearance before "the first gentleman in Europe;" and so far were his musical talents brought to the right market, that from that evening commenced an acquaintance between the Prince and the captain which gradually ripened into an intimate friendship, and as Captain Bloomfield had good manners, good sense, and more tact than falls to most men, lasted while the Prince was king.

For a considerable time the captain was known in fashionable circles as Sir Benjamin Bloomfield, being appointed an Equerry and Gentleman Usher of the Court, and knighted by the Prince in 1815. Two years later, on the retirement of Sir John M'Mahon, he was appointed to the not very laborious offices of Receiver-General of the Duchy of Cornwall, and Private Secretary to the Prince and Keeper of the Privy Purse.

But he had not yet reached to the summit of

the mountain up which his musical talents had led him by an easy ascent. In 1824, as we are told by the Peerages, he was accredited Minister Plenipotentiary and Ambassador Extraordinary to the Court of Stockholm," and shortly afterwards was raised to the Irish Peerage as Lord Bloomfield.

Capt. Gronow, in his amusing and entertaining " Anecdotes and Reminiscences," lets us into a little of the secret history of these last two steps of preferment. He says: " A court intrigue, headed by a fashionable and fascinating marchionesss, caused Sir Benjamin Bloomfield to be sent into splendid exile, this lady attributing to him the fact that she had been compelled to send back to the donor some jewels which had been presented to her by the Prince Regent, but which, as it was afterwards discovered, could not be alienated from the Crown, to which they, in fact, belonged." This was the true reason, then, why Sir Benjamin was sent off as ambassador to Stockholm and eventually created a peer; and such is the real story of the origin of the title.

It is only right to add that, although he had received not a diplomatic but only an ordinary education, Lord Bloomfield's good sense, polished tastes, affable manners, and unostentatious hospitality rendered him exceedingly popular in that northern capital, and that in his " splendid exile" he became as great a favourite with Bernadotte as he had been with the Prince Regent at Windsor, at Brighton, or at Carlton House. The name of Lord Bloomfield (adds Captain Gronow in 1860), is held in great respect even to the present day in Sweden. Eventually he was nominated a Knight Grand Cross of both the Royal Hanoverian Guelphic Order and also of Bath, and promoted to the rank of lieutenant-general in the army and colonel-commandant in the Royal Engineers.

Lord Bloomfield died in the year 1846, at the age of eighty-four, having been twice married. His only son, his issue by his second wife, is the present Lord Bloomfield, who, having followed the diplomatic profession, and having held for many years the post of Minister at the Court of Berlin, has been rewarded with an English peerage, and the dignity of a Knight Grand Cross of the Order of the Bath. Still, however, it may fairly be asserted, I take it, that, in all human probability, these twin coronets would never have been called into existence if it had not been for the occurrence of the chapter of accidents already referred to; and if any moral is to be drawn from the story of Benjamin, Lord Bloomfield, it would seem to be that it is occasionally a profitable investment to give our sons, as well as our daughters, a musical education.

END OF THE FIRST VOLUME.

London : Printed by A. Schulze, 13, Poland Street.